Shirley Mae
of Jangle Creek

by Shirley Mae Heslop

Shirley Heslop

ISBN: 1729611362
ISBN-13: 978-1729611364

DEDICATION

This book is dedicated to my children, grandchildren and great-grandchildren.

ACKNOWLEDGMENTS

I would like to thank my husband, Alan, for putting up with my wondering mind as I contemplated things to write and for encouraging me when things were difficult. Thanks to my niece, Cheryl O'Neill, for a lot of typing. I know it was hard to read my writing at times. Also, I would like to thank my daughter, Hope Harkins, and granddaughter, Rebecca Harkins, for helping me with editing and publication

Shirley Mae

Born in a home near 83 years ago
To a poor farming family, God granted it so.

My life was full of many joys
In a family of six girls three boys.

We wandered the hills in search of flowers
Or splashed away in summer showers.

We rode for hours on our favorite mule
Which later took us to our school.

Slid down the hills, dug in the snow
The days were fun, we loved them so.

Rode ice burgs during the big spring flood
Sometimes rescued by my brother Bud.

Played in the haystack like Little Boy Blue
Forgetting the work Mom said to do.

We fed the chickens, gathered the eggs
Fed the dog but he continued to beg.

We brought in the cows, we herded the sheep,
We better not complain, no not a peep.

We milked the cows, separated the milk
Did the dishes and cooled the milk.

Meals were always a joyous affair
With a wondrous aroma filling the air.

"We're all ready and here" Daddy would say
"Pray Mother", oh how she could pray.

She thanked our Father for being so good
For daily blessing, for our daily food.

She'd ask for His blessing on everyone
And asked in the name of His dear Son.

As we opened our eyes one was sure to say
"Please pass the milk, I'm thirsty today."

Then daddy would glower and grumble away
"We're here for food, not milk'" he'd reply.

Someone was sure to tip over their drink
We're careless young siblings you surely would think.

Then Daddy always had a full cup of tea
He loved it dearly it was plain to see.

He'd sip at it slowly and savor the smell
Then I reached for something, for what I can't tell.

And tipped his cup over, it ran on his lap
He jumped, and he hollered, "You clumsy sap!"

Now Ruth was all mouthy and talked out of turn
"Anyway Daddy tea's good for burns!"

She ran from the room to get out of sight
While we giggled and giggled with all our might.

Daddy was always reading 'bout foods good and bad
"White flour is poison, I'll grind wheat instead."

We grumbled a lot but ate this gross bread
Till Mom put her foot down. "I want white bread
instead."

Then he read the virtues of blackstrap molasses
Take a teaspoon a day or I'll spank your little a**es.

Well I took one taste. T'was enough for me!
He never tasted it once. T'was very plain to see.

We never got a spanking we were promised for sure
It was added to the bread, much better to endure.

We went to school with a team of mules
And here we learned about the golden rule.

With Jack and Jenny and wagon or sleigh
We went each day come what may.

They trudged along through rain or snow
If they got tired it was "We won't go!"

They would stop in their tracks and rest a while
Then when they were rested carry on for a mile.

They were the smartest mules that ever came
After 20 years of school were always the same.

Ephesians 1

Blessed us with blessings
From heaven above,
Chosen us too
Because of His love.

Adopted as children
For His pleasure and will
Accepted and beloved
How our hearts He doth fill.

Redeemed us through blood
Of His blessed Son
Given us wisdom
From this beloved One.

Sealed with the Spirit
Of promise is true.
What an inheritance
For Me and You

Prologue

This book has been a long time in the making. I started it 15 or so years ago when I was in the hospital after having a stroke. I couldn't talk or read. I wanted to use my brain as much as I could to prevent more damage, so I got my husband to bring me up a notebook and pen. I laboured for hours, writing down ideas and things I wanted to say in a book. I couldn't read what I wrote, but Grandpa said it made sense, so I continued writing. It was several years later before, with a lot of effort, I got so I could read again. At first it was only a sentence at a time, then 20 min later another sentence. It was a slow process, but it was progress.

I had on my heart to set to paper a few of the happenings of my life. I do this so you, my children and grandchildren, would know a bit of your family history. It was very different from the life you know it to be now. I also wanted to convey the fact that the Lord was working in my life for many years guiding me along life's path. I want you to know, and be able to picture, what my life was like. When my Mother was about to leave this world to go to a better land, I realized how little I really knew about what her life had really been like. True, I knew she had been born in Minnesota, moved to Brandon, Manitoba then to Melaval, Saskatchewan as a youngster – but what was her life really like? How had the Lord directed her life? I knew very little.

I so yearned to put to paper a few stories of my own life for you; stories that show how the Lord led and directed circumstances in my life. I have been so blessed to have been raised in a home where the Lord was honoured, where my patient, praying Mother was devoted to serving our Lord. Daddy didn't always appear to walk with the Lord until his later years, but I was quite young when he and a neighbour started a Sunday school and a church. He always saw to it that he took us every Sunday. It was here we learned of our need to accept the Lord as Saviour and to serve Him.

My life has not been out of the ordinary, but the Lord used ordinary circumstances to teach me and help me grow to be the person I am today. I have failed many times, but He was always there to help me. He was always there to say, "My strength is made perfect in weakness." This gave me courage to go on.

As I endeavour to put pen to paper, picture a shy little dark haired brown eyed girl, daughter of a poor farming couple, as she started her journey through life. I was raised in the country, far from the city. Even far from the little town, or really should say hamlet, which was 7 miles away. I seldom ever got to go to town. When I found I was able to go to town I would get sick to my stomach in anticipation. I loved the life I lived. I loved the country and farm life. I loved to be with the animals and didn't even mind the work I had to do - like milk cows morning and night.

Finding the Farm – the Early Early Years

1935...Daddy, Jim McPeek, was looking for a place to rent for his growing family. Jim and Dora already had five kids (Evelyn, Ruth, Bud, Irene, and Hazel). He had rented a place at Mazenod, Saskatchewan, but was told he had to move on. It was a distressing time for him, but he got his hay rack out and secured a tent on top and installed an old cook stove and a bed. It was not fancy, but Mom told me it was very comfortable. They loaded all their earthly possessions and started across the country in search of a place. Uncle Charlie, Mom's brother, came along to help. They drove across the country, driving the few head of cattle we had, and the search began. Day after day they trudged along. Mom told me that if she needed bread she would mix up a batch of bread before they started for the day. My older siblings would gather wood and if there was no wood they would gather cow chips which made great fuel for the stove. (cow chips are what they called dried cow droppings that had dried in the sun). When the bread was ready to bake they would stop and fire up the old stove. Before long the aroma of fresh bread floated across the camp.

It was early spring, and a place had to be found before winter came. One day, near Lanigan, Saskatchewan, they came across a little lake. This would be a great place to stop to rest for a few days. Once camp was set up, Daddy set off across country on foot to see what he could find. Mom would bake more bread and make a pot of soup to feed her five hungry children and her brother Charlie which made 8 people to feed. Also, Mom was expecting another baby soon.

Daddy had been walking a long time when he heard music. Daddy was a musician and this music was like a magnet to him. His steps quickened. Before he knew it, he came in sight of a tent. This was where the music was coming from. Entering the tent, he found it was gospel meeting in progress. He sat down and listened. He heard how Jesus Christ had come down from heaven to die for our sins. When the meeting was over he was ready to admit he was a sinner. He repented of his sins and accepted Christ as his Saviour. The preacher asked him where he had come from and Daddy told his story. He was looking for a place to live. "Well," said the preacher, "it is the Lord's day and I don't do business on the Lord's day. Stay here with us for the night and we will talk in the morning." So, Daddy stayed. In the morning the preacher told Daddy he did have a small place we could rent. A deal was struck, and Daddy set off to get his family. Mom was ecstatic to know she would not have to travel any more for a while. She had her hands full with five children to look after and in a month, I was to be born.

(front row: Bud, Evelyn, Irene, and Hazel
back row: Daddy, Shirley, Mom, Ruth)

For two years Daddy worked hard to provide for his growing family. Then one day the landlord came and said, "My son is coming home and wants to live here, so you have to move on." What a blow! Once again, the family set off in search of a place.

(Shirley)

Finally, a place was found in Mazenod, Saskatchewan once again. For two years all was well, but Daddy longed for a place of his own where he could have cattle and farm and never have to move again. He began to look. A realtor told him of a place near Coronach, Saskatchewan. There was a creek and pasture and farm land, but it was poor soil. Many farmers had tried it before and almost starved. So off they went to look at it. When Daddy saw it, it was love at first sight. The lush grass long the creek where there would always be water for cattle was a sight for sore eyes. There was a little shack there too and a tiny barn. The house only had two small rooms but there was an attic and surely, they could make a room up there for the older children to sleep. A deal was struck and soon the plans were made for the move. Daddy, Ruth and Bud drove the cattle there ahead of the rest of the family.

Daddy tried to make things the best he could for when his family came. I am told that potato soup was what they ate day after day. They had potatoes and a cow for milk. Bud didn't like potato soup but soon found out when he got very hungry it was not too bad!

By this time Mom had another baby, Earl. Daddy loaded his family of seven children and Mom in the little old truck he had acquired, and off we set to move to *Jangle Creek* -- as we often called the farm. I remember driving up to the house. I was not quite three years old. Mom was so disappointed. It was nothing but a tar paper shack, but we kids were excited. The tar paper didn't bother us at all. The ladder to the upstairs window was very inviting. Everyone ran for the ladder. Before Daddy could stop us, some were already crawling through the window. "You can't come up, you are too small", I was told by the older kids. But, I was never one to get left behind so I started to climb to prove I could do it just as well as they could. In through the window I crawled and perched on a 2 x 4 truss along with the other kids.

There was no floor in the attic - just 2 x 4 rafters. We had to be careful to only step on the 2 x 4s or we would fall through the ceiling and onto the main floor. This was so exciting! We sat there like a bunch of little birds chattering all at the same time.

The next day Daddy went to town for beautiful wood for a floor and stairs. It was just pine tongue-and-groove wood but to me it was beautiful. I watched with amazement as Daddy made stairs to the attic and stairs to the basement (which was just a dirt hole under the house). What a smart Daddy I had! I watched for hours. I didn't care to go out and investigate the yard. I watched as Daddy measured and sawed and nailed until at last he said I could try the stairs out. I felt like a real princess walking up those fancy stairs. Now boards were carried up and laid out and nailed down. We now had a floor. What a beautiful room! Beds were set up and we 5 girls had our own nice bedroom. This was luxury.

Life at Jangle Creek Farm

At night we could hear a booming noise outdoors. It was really an American Bittern, but Daddy used to tell us it was a "ding-mall". He was a monster and came out at night and had a flaming fiery tongue and looked like a big dinosaur. It was a horrible thing to have to go to the outhouse after dark with a "ding-mall" prowling around. You might ask 'What is an outhouse'? - it is a toilet, a small little building that was built over a hole in the ground. Inside was a bench, with two holes. This is where you sat to do your business.

School

I loved my freedom and I loved to roam the hills with my brother Earl. I knew where each kind of flower grew and when they were ready to open. As they lifted their heads and opened their pretty petals to the sun shine I was there to carefully pick a few to take back to my mother. She would put them in a glass jar and place in the center of the table. She didn't even seem to mind that all too often tiny bugs would climb out of the flowers and onto the table top.

I loved the little kittens in the barn and spent hours petting their soft little bodies. They would nestle in my arms and purr happily. Then, of course, there were the little calves and lambs to play with too. Oh, life was far too busy and fun to have to spend it in school.

Yes, I loved my freedom. So why did I have to go to school I asked? Daddy assured me it was because he didn't want me to grow up to be a dunce. Yes," if I never went to school", he said, "Indeed I would be a dunce."

I would soon be 6 years old and that meant I would have to start school. So, all summer long I was a bundle of nerves, and I heard in my mind, "There are only a few days left and you will have to go to school." I heard it as I waded in the creek. I heard it as old Jenny's hooves pounded the dirt as I bounced along on her back. I heard it as the dust rose from the dirt as my little feet ran across the yard and even while I petted my favourite little soft kitten. It echoed in my mind from early morning to late at night as I climbed into my bed and tried to go to sleep. So, when August 8th came I was panic stricken. To make matters worse it was to begin on my birthday.

I was determined I would not go! Not at all! But I was told in no uncertain terms that on my sixth birthday I would be going to school. The sight of Daddy's razor strap on the wall told me I would be going! School always started early in August, so we could be off at Christmas until nearly February when the worst weather was passed. No matter what I did I could not forget that the time was soon coming when I had to go to school.

A Country School

The country school had grades one to ten
And a grade missing every now and then.

We learned to sing, to quote, to speak
And in the ball game to compete.

But most of all we learned to read
To understand math's complex creed.

We learned to share and to make friends
When we offend to make amends.

Did a lot of learning, a lot of fun too
And in the classroom gum not to chew.

Under the desktop it would be stowed
Or on the end of your nose it must go.

We learned a lot that is for sure
When tough times come we must endure.

But more important it seems to me
Was what we learned at my mother's knee.

There was a little one room school house, Mountain Cedar School, we were all to attend. I was very shy and going to school seemed very scary to me. I was afraid of being there with so many kids that I didn't know, and all last year the kids came home from school with horror stories of how mean the teacher, Miss Stewart, was. She was very strict and screamed and applied the strap very often. It took very little to get her angry, and then she used the strap without mercy.

So, on the morning of August the 8th, excitement was in the air. All six of us got ready for school and with breakfast over we picked up our dinner pails and headed out to the wagon. Faithful old Jack and Jenny waited to carry us across the grassy hills to the little one room school house sitting there on the bald prairie. Evelyn, Ruth, Bud, Irene, Hazel and I got in to the wagon and off we went, bouncing along as the mules trudged across the creek and over the bumpy trail heading across country to school.

I was so shy. It was awful that first day. When we got to school I didn't know what to do. I was so frightened that I just stood there not knowing what I was expected to do or where to go. What was going to happen to me today? Evelyn took charge. She lovingly took my hand and took me in to the school and showed me where to hang my coat. Then after placing my dinner pail on the floor under where my coat neatly hung, she showed me the little desk, where I would sit. Once I was settled in my desk she went to the other side of the room to where the big desks were and sat down. I was a proud that my big sister had carefully placed me in my seat before she sat down. It made me feel very special. She was the best big sister a girl could ask for. It was then that a chubby little lady stood up in the front of the room and announced, "My name is Mrs. Henderson. I will be your new teacher this year." I had to admit that even though I was frightened, she didn't look a bit scary like Miss Stewart had been. Mrs. Henderson was an older lady who lived close by. She even looked like she might be nice. Perhaps school would not be so bad after all. It didn't take long for me to find out that school was not so bad. I settled in and even enjoyed it a bit.

At recess and noon hour we played group games. The game area was between the barn and the school. The area was divided in half and there was a round circle goal drawn in each side. One goal was near the school and one was near the barn. We loved to play "steal sticks". In each goal we placed 10 sticks. All of the kids got to play. We were divided equally, and the idea was to sneak across the center line to the goal to steal a stick and return to your goal without getting caught. If you were tagged, you were put in the goal along with the sticks as prisoner. The idea was to steal all of the sticks out of your opponent's goal. I was so small they put me to guard the goal. The big boys, from the other team, would sneak up and say, "If you tag me I will spank you because it is your birthday." (You know, a spank for every year old you are, and a pinch to grow an inch.) Well, they had stolen almost all of our sticks before my sister, Ruth, found out what the boys were doing and came to my rescue.

The schoolhouse was about three miles from our farm. It was called Mountain Cedar. I think it was named that because the hill it was beside was covered with creeping cedar. Oh, how proud we were of our school. We were sure it was the best school in the country. It was a little one room school house with one teacher. Often, she had at least one student in each grade up to grade 8. Grade 9 and 10 attended as well, but they took correspondence courses. She only helped them when she had time. It was a big job to teach so many different classes.

The school room was about 30' square with high windows on 3 sides. They definitely were not meant for little people like me to look out. The front wall was all black board. Above the center black board hung a set of maps which the teacher would roll down when she was teaching history or to show us where places were that the news talked about. The teacher would often write assignments on the boards for us to do. At the front of the room was the teacher's desk. Students sat facing her in desks that ranged from small on one side and big ones on the other side of the room. Along the back were coat hooks for us to hang coats on. Dinner pails and boots were to be carefully placed under the hook with our name on it. That was the plan, but we were not always good at keeping it neat. Girls' hooks were on one side, and the boys were to use the hooks on the other side. We girls usually had no trouble finding our mittens, because we put them with our coats. On the other hand, the boys often had to scramble to find their lost mitts, or even a misplaced boot or cap.

At one side at the back of the room, there was a sand table. How we loved to play in the sand. When we studied the Canadian Indians, we made Indian villages. Lakes were made with glass placed over blue paper. Teepees were made with cloth covering a frame made of twigs and toy horses were placed with a travois propped up and bundles of leather like things were placed on them to look like the Indians were carrying buffalo furs. We even made an Indian grave and piled little stones on top like the Indians did when someone died. When we studied the early explorers, we made a map of Canada showing the Great Lakes and the rivers. That way we were able to visualize better the trails the early explorers took. History had come to life!

————

Most of the time we went to school by mule team. In the summer we had a big heavy wagon, not a nice buggy. In the winter we had the same wagon but with sleigh runners under it instead of wheels. When I was about nine, Dad made a sleigh that he called a "jumper". He called it that, because when the horses ran, it jumped from snow bank to snow bank. It was a rough ride. We didn't worry about that though, because our mules, Jack and Jenny, never ran. In fact, we never even had to drive them. We tied the reins to the post on the front of the wagon while we nestled in the straw or wrestled in the wagon. In the winter when our feet got too cold, we ran along beside the sleigh to get the blood circulating again. Then we would climb back in and snuggle back in the straw.

The trail that we took went through the creek and cut across our pasture, and then across the prairie hills to the school. The last few years, the farmers started to farm the land, and we had to go on the trails between fields. This didn't make us very happy. We loved the prairie and wild flowers, which were being eaten up by wheat fields. It also took us longer to get to school. It made us very sad as year after year the neighbours would plow up another field. Our beautiful prairie was disappearing.

One day, we were wrestling, and we tipped the sleigh over on its side. The doubletree came off and we were shocked! The team just walked off a few feet and waited for us to reconnect it. We walked to the far side of the sled, tipped it back over, and then hooked the mules back up. When we realized that we were in sight of home, we were really scared. We thought that Dad would be mad, but he surprised us and only laughed.

The teacher set up a cleaning schedule. Everyone was assigned chore to do. When it was your turn you had to sweep the floors and clean the blackboard and brushes before you went home.

There was no well at the schoolhouse. Our family was the one that had to bring the drinking water. Each morning we hurried with milking the cows before having breakfast. Then we grabbed our syrup tin dinner pails, bundled up warm and headed to the well for water. We would fill a cream can with nice clear spring water, then we all piled in to the wagon and off the mules headed.

The mules knew the way, so we didn't have to pay attention to where we were headed. When we came to a gate they would stop until someone opened it, then walk through, and wait while we closed the gate. Then they would continue to trudge across the open prairie to the school.

Once we got to school, we took the water can into the schoolroom, removed the lid and hung on a long-handled dipper. We all drank out of the same dipper when we were thirsty until I was about 8 years old. Then there was a lot of talk about of germs so each of us brought our own cup. We hung them on nails on the wall with our name above them. The girls were very careful to use their own cup, but some of the boys were lazy, and would just grab the nearest cup to use. Of course, they only did this when they thought no one was looking so that they didn't get into trouble.

––––––––

When we got to school in the winter the furnace had always gone out and all the ink bottles would be frozen solid. In the centre of the school room floor was a 2' square register. The school had a basement with cement walls and dirt floor. There was a bin of coal for the furnace in one corner. The furnace was just a big stove surrounded by tin so that the heat went up to the floor vent above. There was a two-foot square register vent on the classroom floor to let the heat up to the schoolroom from the furnace. This provided all of the heat that we had. In the winter, it was our family's job to get the furnace going, so that it was warm in the school when the rest got there.

As soon as the warm air started to come up through the register in the school room, we loved to stand over the register and soak up the heat. As the heat blew up through the vent, it made our skirts puff out like a hot air balloon. Or sometimes, I would imagine I was a princess dressed in a beautiful long dress that was all lace and ruffles. Then the teacher would ring the bell and say, "Take your seats." I was brought back to reality. Once again just a poor little girl who was dressed in secondhand clothes and was very cold.

When it was time to start school, we put our ink bottles on the register to thaw and took our seats. For the first hour, until our ink was thawed, we had to use a pencil. We didn't have ballpoint pens then. We used stick pens, which were a pencil-like stick with a pen nib stuck into it. After every word or two we would have to dip the pen into the ink bottle for more ink. Until you got good at it, the pen would leave ink blobs on your paper and you would end up with ink all over your fingers. I had blue fingers a lot of the time. I finally got better at it, however, and could keep the ink from getting on my fingers.

One day one of the boys didn't loosen the lid on his ink bottle when he set it on the register. When the bottle got hot, it exploded, and made a huge ink spot on the ceiling. The teacher was upset and made us wash the ceiling. We washed for days, standing on the top of the piano. I am sure that it made a big mess on the piano top. When daddy finally heard what we were doing the teacher nearly lost her job. She was being hired to teach not clean. That ended the scrubbing. That didn't hurt our feelings a bit because after the first day we found out that scrubbing was very hard work.

In the winter we used to also put containers of cocoa and soup on the register when school began so we that we could have a hot lunch. Often, we had soup. Mom used to take a can of tomato soup and add at least 2 cans of milk and sometimes more. The neighbour kids' mom only added one can of milk. I used to feel so sorry for them having a mom that was so wasteful. Besides that, our soup tasted much better, with the extra milk. Sometimes we would also put potatoes on top of the register to bake for lunch. This was real luxury.

I was always small. The window at school was too high for me to see out. One day I got in trouble because of it. There was an escaped convict on the loose, named Sheffield. The police seemed unable to catch him. Every day the stories grew bigger. He was reported to have a white half-ton truck. The police, it was rumoured, went on some very wild chases across the country, but were unable to catch him. I was terrified, and imagined Sheffield was lurking in every dark corner and behind every bush. One day at school, I heard a truck go by. Since I was in grade one, my desk was just under the window. I just had to see if it was Sheffield, so I stood on my tiptoes. I was still too short to see out of the window, so I climbed up on my desk seat. I still couldn't see, so I stood on my desktop and stood on my lunch pail to see out. Sure enough, there was a pickup going by, followed by billows of dust. Was it white? I couldn't make out the colour because of the billows of dust that surrounded it.

Just then Mrs. Henderson yelled – "Shirley!" She startled me, and I scampered down. She took me up to the front. Since she was busy, and didn't know what to do with me, she shoved me under her desk, pulled her chair up, and sat down. There wouldn't have been room for me if I hadn't been so small, but there I huddled. I curled up in a tight little ball, so that I would be as far from her knees as I could. Then she forgot about me. I spent all afternoon under the desk with nothing to do but stare at her fat knees. I was so humiliated. Mrs. Henderson discovered me there at the end of the day. I think that she felt bad for having forgotten me there. But you can be sure that I never stood on my desk again.

Halloween

Soon it was Thanksgiving and then came Halloween. We had no idea Halloween was connected to occult. Witches were just pretend or, so we thought. We just didn't know. So, we did all we could to have a fun time. Usually the party was in the evening. We all dressed up as scary as we could. The older kids always had a haunted house fixed up. It was made by hanging sheets to make walls. We were blindfolded then they stuck our hands into chicken feet and slimy jelly, while they talked in a scary voice about it being body parts off of a corpse. It was gross! I didn't like it but we all went in anyway and screamed at the appropriate times. Then we bobbed for apples. Apples were floating in a tub of water and we had to hold our hands behind our back and pick the apples up with our teeth. My mouth was so small I never did get one to eat. One year a neighbour boy stuck his head in the water and fetched an apple for my girlfriend and me. He was our hero that night. As usual the mothers served coffee and all kinds of yummy food.

Our Christmas Concert

Once Halloween was over we started to plan for the Christmas concert. The teacher had looked for weeks for plays and poems for us to learn. We also spent a lot of time practicing singing. We sang songs like *Silent Night, Away in a Manger,* and *We Three Kings.* They were mostly songs about the Lord Jesus. No one in our school could be unclear about the wonders of the birth of our Lord. Since our family made up most of the school, no one complained about it.

All our spare time was spent making decorations and planning costumes for plays. A few days before the concert some of the parents would come and put up a small platform for us to stand on. A wire was strung across the room and a curtain was hung. Excitement was in the air.

Finally, the day came. We dressed in our best clothes and shone our shoes and we girls curled our hair. We girls always wanted a new dress for the concert. Evelyn helped by making some. One by one we marched onto the stage to recite our poems or perform a play.

Some of the skits and songs were really funny. One I remember was a song – Hazel and Angela (a neighbour) sang. They were a husband and wife who were black. They were sitting on a log. He (Hazel) kept singing to the girl (Angela) proposing marriage. He sang of all the things he would do for her or give her if she would only marry him. She would answer "no not even for all that". Then he would sing again offering her more and she kept singing back "No she would not marry him." It was really quite funny. The funniest part though was when they tried to get the shoe polish off their faces after the play was over. Their faces were pretty red and sore from the scrubbing, and even then, it didn't all come off. For the remainder of the concert they had smudged faces.

We always had a drill. The one I remember best was the one where we were all dressed like dolls, with ruffled pinafores and bonnets. We didn't have enough girls so my younger brother, Earl, had to dress like one. Oh, he didn't like that! He refused to take off his pants,

(Shirley is 3rd from the left, Hazel, Earl on the far right)

but he put the pinafore on top. His pant legs showed out the bottom. He was such a good sport to do it. We marched back and forth crisscrossing the stage to music about dolls. We walked stiff legged because dolls don't bend their knees.

We always acted out the story of the birth of Jesus too. For this all of the kids were involved. Some were shepherds, wise men, angels, and of course Mary and Joseph. One of my dolls (Sharon Marie) was used as baby Jesus. Someone always read the story about the Lord's birth from the Bible. Then Daddy played his fiddle while we sang a bunch of carols about the Lord Jesus. After all, we wanted to remember who was born so many years ago.

We younger ones always had poems we had to memorize and quote. I really hated that. Daddy always made us practice at home. When we looked shy or twisted the corner of our skirt or twisted our hair, because we were nervous, he would imitate us to show us how silly it looked. He wanted us to look confident. He used to say – "look everyone in the eye, as if they owed you $10, then you won't be so scared." It was hard, but it was good experience for us.

As the last of the program was done we sat in anticipation, then sure enough we hear a "HO HO HO" and Santa came running in. He passed out the gifts from under the tree. We had drawn names and brought gifts for each other. He also gave out candy bags. One year I got in real trouble. I recognized who Santa was, so I told my friends. "Daddy is Santa Claus." Were their moms ever mad! The kids still believed in Santa Claus. I was so disgusted! How could anyone believe Santa could come down a chimney anyway? When Santa was done with the gifts he ran out. He took off his suit and put it in a box which went up into the dusty attic until next year.

The ladies then got the refreshments ready – wonderful sandwiches and all kinds of fancy cakes and cookies, and of course lots of coffee. We ate a bit but mostly stuffed our faces with candy from our bags. By the time lunch was served it was time to head home. The men got the horses hooked to the sleighs and loaded us all in and off we went. Mom sat on a box in the straw, holding her youngest child and we girls cuddled close to her. As the horse started off on the run someone started to sing. So, we sang at the top of our voices nestled in the straw at Mom's feet as she sat holding our youngest sibling. Snow glistened in the moonlight. Our horses didn't have bells, but the harnesses jingled as they ran – what a beautiful sound! I feel a bit homesick when I think about it. Life was good.

———

One year I needed new shoes. Mom ordered them from Eaton's catalogue, but they never came and never came. That was the year we had so much snow the telephone poles were almost covered. Trains were not getting through either. Some places they had a chain of men up the snow bank. The first one would throw the snow to the second one, and the second one would throw to the third one etc. After about six men it finally got to the top of the bank. The snow kept coming. It seemed like the snow would never stop. One morning after a big storm we got up and got ready to go milk the cows. When we stepped out the door we got the shock of our life. The barn was nowhere to be seen. We went back in and said, "Mom we can't find the barn!" She was very cross because she thought we were just fooling around. We finally got her to come look for herself. Sure enough, the barn was completely covered with snow. "I do dee-clare!" she said. The men had to dig down to the barn door and carve steps for us to walk down to the cows. They carried a lot of water for the animals to drink for days. Then they dug bigger steps, so the horses could climb the steps to get out. The cows never saw the outside of the barn for weeks and weeks.

I prayed and prayed that my shoes would come. The day before the concert, Daddy came home from town with a parcel from Eaton's. My shoes had arrived. I was so proud to walk on stage with new shiny shoes. I thanked the Lord many times for answering my prayer.

―――――――

No more school for six weeks! But just because there was no more school, didn't mean we could sleep in. The cows needed to be milked. Since we had a hard time getting up we went to bed early – right? Wrong! We didn't like to go to bed either. After chores were done, the supper dishes washed, and the milk separated and put downstairs to cool we had the evening to enjoy. We usually gathered in the kitchen around the old cook stove. Mom left the oven door open which gave us more heat and often one of us would perch ourselves on it. The heat felt so good on our backs. Mom usually had her mending, Daddy would be reading his mystery books while most of us girls had our embroidery work and the boys often played board games.

––––––––––

During our winter break we spent a lot of time in the snow. One year there was so much snow we dug a lot of tunnels, but Mom was worried they would cave in on us, so we didn't make them too long.

Valentine's Day and other holidays

All too soon it was the end of January and school was ready to start again. Back to getting up earlier while it was still dark, stumbling to the barn in the dark guided only by the light of the old coal oil lantern. Back to hurrying with breakfast, making lunches, hitching up the old mules and stopping by the well for water before we headed three miles across country to school. After the first couple of days we got caught up in making plans for a valentine party. We each had to make a box to put on our desks for valentines. We girls tried to make ours the nicest in the school. Most of the boys were content with an old shoe box.

We had to give everyone a valentine, so we picked the least mushy ones and grudgingly dropped them in the boys' boxes. Often, we would gasp as we opened our boxes when we found a mushy one from a boy we disliked a great deal. Sometimes, for a treat, we got fancy and made heart shaped cookies and iced them. These the boys would eat as fast as they could. I kept wondering, "Why can't they at least eat slowly and enjoy them? It took a lot of work and time to make them and the boys eat them in one bite!"

The next excitement was St. Patrick's Day. We usually never had a party but read Irish poems and made shamrocks for decoration. One year, the teacher had a bright idea. My sister Irene was getting married, so she said, "We should have a St. Patrick's Day program and invite all the parents. That way they would all be here, and we could turn it into a wedding shower for Irene." We were so excited. We learned all the Irish tunes we could and read poems and everything we could that was Irish. When we were all done our program, the community put on a mock wedding. That was the first Irene knew that the shower was for her. Evelyn dressed

up like a Bride – with a curtain for a headdress and veil. Lester McLeod played the groom. The person playing the minister was dressed up with a pillow stuffed in his shirt to give him a big belly, and glasses hung almost at the end of his nose. The "minister" went through the vows and dropped the rings and had to get on his hands and knees to find them. We all laughed until tears ran down our faces. Then of course came the gifts and the big array of food and coffee.

Pie Social

In the spring one year we decided our school really needed to raise money for the Red Cross. We were very aware of all the good the Red Cross did because we heard what they did to help soldiers during the war. After a lot of discussions, we decided to have a pie social. At a pie social, the ladies and girls all made a pie and put it in a fancy box. No one is supposed to know whose box it is. I worked for weeks making a fancy box for my pie. After an evening of games, they would auction off the boxes. Whoever bought your box was the one you'd eat it with. I didn't like that at all, but I had to be a good sport. Someone got clued in which box was mine and bid it up quite high. A guy I didn't like at all bought it. The boy I really liked sat right behind us. I couldn't eat much so we shared it with him. The boy who bought my pie wasn't happy to have to share, but "them's the breaks." I thought it was quite funny because my pie sold for four times what my teacher's pie did.

———

We almost never missed school. We took pride in the fact that we were very healthy. But one winter I had a week off. One day we girls decided we needed a bath. We could not bring in the big tub from outside like we usually did since Mom was cooking and the men were coming in and out all afternoon. We decided to take a wash basin in the living room and cuddle around the pot belly stove and keep warm while bathing. All was well until I bent over to dry myself after my bath and my bum hit the side of the red-hot heater. Then the screaming started. I was so humiliated to have to let Daddy put ointment on the burn and bandage it up. For days I could not sit at all. I stood to eat meals and lay down on the couch when I got tired of standing. But the hard part was when Daddy wrote a note to the teacher telling her why I was not in school. Hazel said that she read the note and just smiled. I was so embarrassed! She may have thought it funny, but I didn't. I was very glad when I could sit again and go back to school.

———

Traveling to and from school in bad weather was dangerous, but Daddy always said if we were in the sleigh the mules would bring us home. However, one day we were dropped off at school and were to walk home. It was very cold out, but walking would warm us some. By mid-afternoon the wind got up. Mr. Kupper came to pick up his kids before the storm got any stronger. The teacher said she would ride along with him since she lived close by. What was she to do with us? We were told to get dressed and head out.

We had just gotten out of the school yard when the wind picked up and we could not see our hand in front of our face. Would we be found in the morning frozen to death in a snow bank? We gathered together and took council. Irene and Hazel decided we should line up in a row. Irene would lead, and Hazel would follow last. I was in the middle and in charge of Earl. If he fell I was to get him up, but he was my job to care for. Irene faced the storm as long as she could stand it then, she and Hazel would trade places. Every couple of minutes Irene would call, "Are you okay?" Earl would call to me, and I would call to Hazel, and we would call back one by one until Irene got the message we were all okay. Many times, the message went back and forth. I kept praying, "Please Lord get us home safely and help us not to freeze to death in the snow bank." Each snow bank we plodded through I thought I couldn't go any farther. My legs were so tired, and we were all so cold. Finally, we came to the top of the valley. The storm let up a little bit and we could see where we were. We were off track but now we knew we could make it home. What rejoicing there was when we finally arrived. We were happy because we were so cold and tired. Mom had thought she could have possibly lost four of her children.

The Creek

As spring came the snow would melt and leave an inch of water on top of the ice. It would freeze and leave a layer of water under a thin layer of ice. This we called "rubber ice". One Sunday morning Earl and I, and our cousin, Bill, were having a great time on it and were totally ignoring the fact that we were supposed to be in the house getting ready for Sunday school. All of a sudden, the ice gave way and we all fell in. It was in a part of the creek we didn't know how deep it was. We were sure we were going to drown. Much to our relief we were only waist deep when we touched bottom. We scrambled out of the creek and ran to the house soaking wet. Now, we were sure we would get sympathy. We didn't. We got bawled out and didn't even get help getting dry clothes.

School was out for us because of floods. Since we couldn't get to school we had time to play. As the creek flooded, the ice began to crack, and float down the stream. We had fun jumping on a piece of ice and floating along. As long as it stayed close to shore we were okay. One day we got an idea – why don't we use the old stone boat. It was wood so would float. We played Tom Sawyer. All was well until it started to go too far, and we couldn't get to shore to pull it back. So, we did what kids are good at – we yelled, "Help". Walt came to our rescue, took a horse out and grabbed the rope and pulled us back. Then of course we got a stern lecture, from Daddy, of the dangers of water during spring flood. That slowed us down for a couple of days then we went right back playing by the creek.

The creek held its charms. We knew every inch of it. Some places were deep, but most places were shallow enough to wade in when it wasn't flooded. I didn't like to wade much because the mud bottom was so squishy, and you never knew what was hidden in it – tin cans, broken bottles, etc. But then again, I was squeamish about the mud bottom and the bloodsuckers in the weeds we had to wade through to get to deep enough water to swim. I much preferred rafting. We gathered boards from all over and made some great rafts and poled ourselves up and down the creek. On very hot days we used to go swimming. Mom gave us each a pillowcase. We put two syrup pails in the pillow cases, with the lids on tight, and we tied the pillowcase closed. (homemade water wings). We lay on the pillowcase contraption with

a can under each arm and it floated us beautifully.

Chores

When it was time to milk, the cows had to be brought in to the barn. We could call – "*come Boss, come Boss*" and they came if they were close enough, but often they were too far to hear so we had to go get them. As usual we were barefoot. Usually we had to walk across the alkali flats where there were lots of mud puddles to walk through. It felt so good to have the warm soft mud squish between our toes. We even caught a little killdeer bird a time or two, but usually they could run too fast. Sometimes as we hopped from mud puddle to mud puddle to avoid walking on the sharp grass, a snake would slither by. Then you should have seen me run….. ….. When out getting the cows, I had to stop every five minutes to pick the prickles out of my feet. The little bit of grass that grew around the mud puddles had a sharp point on top. It was hard on the feet, but we found if we picked it carefully we could make necklaces by taking the pointed end and push it into the hollow stem. Sometimes we made very long chains and pretended they were fancy jewelry.

———

We handled the cows so much that they got pretty tame. We often climbed on their backs and went for a ride. It was hard though because many of them were pregnant and so round that our little legs didn't go down their sides enough to hang on. We often fell off.

We spent a lot of time playing but always we had to milk the cows, morning and night. I think the job I hated most was washing the milk separator (*photo - right*). Every morning, after we used it, we had to take it all apart, wash it and put it back together ready for use after evening milking. All the little disks inside had to be taken apart and washed individually. What a job! It would not be such a job now with lots of hot running water, but we didn't have that. We had to carry water in from the well and heat it on the old cook stove before we could begin washing.

Once a week we had to churn butter. (*photo of butter churn, previous page*) If the cream was cool it didn't take too long, but it seemed like a long time. It was rewarding in a way because once it was churned we would run for a glass, drain off some buttermilk, add salt and pepper and drink. Fresh buttermilk is so good! For a while Mom used a butter press (*photo bellow*) and made pounds of butter to sell. It was a lot of work for a few pennies, but we were very poor, so it was good to get the income.

Later she decided it was better just to sell the cream to Johnson Dairy in Moose Jaw. Once a week she would pour all the cream into a cream can and put it on the train to ship to Moose Jaw.

One summer we girls decided we wanted to earn some money. The only thing we came up with was shipping cream. So, Mom made a deal with us. We milked every cow that would let us milk her. I think we milked 14 cows. Boy, that took a lot of work! I don't think we ever did end up with any money, but it was fun to dream about it anyway. (*photo previous page - cream can*)

(photo – cook stove)

Laundry was another big job. In the early days, Mom washed on a scrub board, and then she wrung the

water out by hand, and hung the clothes on the line to dry. Most of the clothes were first put into a boiler on the cook stove, with handmade soap. Mom stoked the fire to heat the water up to be very hot. This, along with the homemade soap, helped to loosen the dirt from the clothes. Then, the clothes were put into a tub and scrubbed on a board (*photo above*) until they were clean, then rinsed, and wrung out and hung to dry.

After a few years, Daddy found a washing machine for mom to use (*photo below*). This was so much easier to wash clothes. I well remember this machine. It was like a 1/2 of cylinder or a barrel with a handle that stuck up from the side at the centre. The tub was latched tightly in place while the water was added, and then the soap and clothes. Once the clothes were added and the lid closed, we took the handle and pushed it back and forth, back and forth agitating the clothes inside. It was not hard to do at first, but after the first few minutes it got really tiring to do and our arms got very exhausted. The movement of the machine agitated the clothes and moved water through them, dirt was released, and unless the clothes were really, really dirty, it took about 5 min to wash a load. No scrubbing on the scrub board was needed except for very dirty items. Behind the machine we had a tub of clear water. When we decided the clothes were clean, we latched

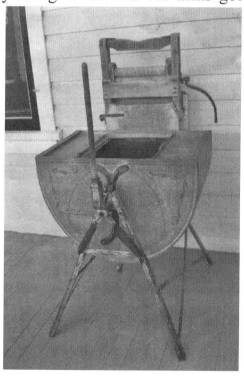

the machine in place, so the tub wouldn't move, opened the lid, and fed the clothes through the hand-turned wringer and into the rinse water. We then agitated them more in the rinse water by hand to get all the soapy water out of them and put them through the wringer again. They were then ready to hang outside to dry. This machine was wonderful and so much easier than the scrub board and hand wringing the clothes. Once the clothes were all washed, the machine was latched again to secure it and a bucket was placed under the front side, where there was a tap, to drain the water out. It took two or three 5 gal buckets to drain out all the dirty water, which was then carried outside and dumped.

Summer time was easy to dry the clothes. Clothes lines were hung from 2 heavy poles in the yard. On windy days they dried very quickly and smelled so fresh, and the clothes were nice and soft from flapping in the wind. Winter time was more difficult. Most of the time,

mom still hung the clothes outside for a couple of hours. It was a very cold job and her hands would freeze while she did this, but the frost seemed to take some of the moisture out of the clothes. Then we brought them inside and lay them on the table to thaw as they were frozen stiff as boards. We were very careful not to bend them while they were frozen because they would break. Once they thawed, mom hung them on lines that stretched across the living room - 5 or 6 lines of clothes filled the room. She also had a clothes horse, which was a wooden rack that folded up for storage when not in use. This is where she put small things, like shorts and underwear and socks. Once the clothes were

frozen on the clothes horse (see photo), she just had to bring it in and stand it in the kitchen near the stove. They were there until they were dry, which was usually the next day. Underneath the lines that were hung in the living room, was a wonderful place to play. I can still smell the smell of fresh laundry drying.

The next day was ironing day. We didn't have steam irons, so the clothes had to be laid out and we took our hand, dipped into a dish of water and sprinkled water all over the clothes to dampen them. Then each piece of clothing was rolled up and placed into a tub. Then another one was sprinkled and rolled and placed on top of it, until all the pieces we were going to iron were in the tub. It took a few hours for the moisture to spread through all the material. The little bit of dampness would create steam during the ironing process. Then, the real job started. Irons (*photo below*) were lined on the hot part of the stove. We got really good at snapping a handle on an iron, turning it over, wetting our finger and touching the iron. We could tell if it was hot enough or too hot to use just by touching it with our wet finger. By wetting our finger, it kept the iron from burning us. When the iron got too cold to work well, the iron was placed back on the stove, and the handle was removed, and a second iron was taken up to use.

All of the cotton shirts and dresses had to be starched. We did this by taking a pan with water, heating

it and adding cornstarch. Experience taught us how much starch to add. When done correctly, the shirts and dresses were beautifully crisp once they were ironed. Clothes were dipped in the starch mixture and hung to dry, then sprinkled, and then ironed.

It was often said, 'people can tell how good a housekeeper a woman was by the whites on her clothes lines.' If her towels (which were most times made from bleached flour sacks) were really white, she was praised.

Later years Daddy found a gas-powered washing machine, but the motor had to be installed on the front step, and the front door left open and the belt ran into the house where Mom had her machine sitting in the kitchen/porch. It was ok for summer use but too cold to use in the winter time.

Soap? Most of the soap we used, Mom made. I am not sure how she made it, because she and Evelyn made it when we were at school, but I know that she used beef tallow (fat) and lye. It was made in the big boiler and placed on the cook stove. It took most of the day to make a batch. When it was done cooking, the soap was placed in flat pans to cool and get hard, then before it got too hard she cut it into squares about 4" sq. This soap really did a great job of removing the dirt from the clothes, and a batch lasted for a long time. I can still remember the strong smell of it.

The well

All of our drinking water had to be carried in a bucket from the well. The well was ¼ mile from the house, over the hill and down by the spring. Daddy dug it by hand. It was about 3' square and 3' deep. He made a wooden cribbing around it and a wooden lid. When we wanted water, we had to run down the path, tie a rope on the pail and drop it down the well. When it filled with water we pulled it up and carried it to the house.

One summer I had a problem. My friend had given me a broach. It was a pink bunny, but it didn't have a proper clasp. It had a straight pin like Remembrance Day poppies do. So, I would wear it with care. One day I got out my bunny and proudly pinned it on. I walked around so proudly. I was a lady with beautiful jewelry! However, after awhile, I forgot I had it on. A few hours later I remembered – I felt for it – and it was gone. I had lost my one and only treasured jewelry. I looked and looked for it. I walked everywhere I could remember that I had been, but no luck. I prayed, "Lord please help me find my broach." Then Mom called "Please, I need some water." So, reluctantly, I grabbed the buckets and headed to the well. As I walked down the path the dry dirt squished up between my toes. How could I live without my beautiful broach? I arrived at the well and lifted the lid, snapped the bucket onto the rope and began to lower the water pail. The sun shone down and guess what I saw laying on the sand at the bottom of the well – my beautiful bunny. I got the water for Mom then tried to reach down but my arms were far too short. All the way to the house I thought of how I could reach my broach. Then I thought – I bet the hoe would pick it up. So, I ran as fast as my little legs would carry me back to the well, hoe in hand. I carefully put the hoe down and scooped up my bunny. I stopped right there and prayed a little prayer of thanks to God for answering my prayer. I still have that bunny today.

Our Meat

One summer a bunch of the farmers (I think about a dozen families) got together and organized a beef club. Each week one of them would supply an animal to butcher. One farmer had a little shed he could use as a meat house, so he butchered the beef and cut it up. Then we all went and got our meat for the week. All summer it was our job to hitch up the mules to the wagon and drive the three miles to Mr. Tottons' and get our meat. It was hot out and the flies were plentiful, but we wrapped our meat in towels and hurried home to get it in the icebox. It took us all morning to go over and back. This club didn't last long. Daddy thought that he was getting the worst cuts of meat so decided to back out. I think that the others lost interest after a while too.

For some reason Mom didn't mind if meat got frozen. The thought of the time was that if vegetables were frozen they became poisonous. I guess that didn't apply to meat. Come fall they used to kill a beast and let it hang from a teepee-like structure for 2-3 weeks. Usually it was cool enough in the fall in Saskatchewan to keep it from spoiling. It used to cool off pretty steadily in the fall. Then the meat was brought in to a small bunkhouse that the hired hand slept in come summer. Here it was away from the cats and Mom would bring it in as needed. The only way beef could be kept during the summer was to rub it very, very well in smoke salt and then hang it in the stairway to the basement to keep it as cool as possible.

In the summer, Sunday dinner was usually roast chicken or Mom would cut a chicken up and roll it in flour to brown it, then put it in a pot and cook it. Either way chicken was almost always served Sundays in the summer. Saturdays we baked pies and caught a chicken and cleaned it and then cleaned the house. This happened almost every Saturday. Sunday was special and often, once we girls got older, so we could help, we often had company on Sunday. In the winter Sunday dinner was often a beef roast or a turkey.

Horses

Horseback riding was a big part of our summer. We always took Jenny, our mule, and sometimes Nelly, our dapple-gray, horse. I always wanted a saddle on Jenny because, if she didn't have a saddle on, when we got to a nice soft piece of dirt she would lay down and roll. Then we had to jump off quickly but jump on just as fast as she was getting up, or we couldn't get back on her. The horses were both good with kids and sometimes we rode 3 or 4 on at one time. We had a very big pasture and would ride for miles. At one corner of our pasture we once found an old Indian campground. We could see the circles of stones they put around the bottom of their teepees. Then there were piles of stones – 6' long 2' wide. We decided they must be graves. That scared us so badly that we headed for home as fast as the horses could go. We never went there again. We did go to the other end of the pasture and go under the bridge to a big pasture we called the Hudson Bay. That was because it used to belong to a company called the Hudson Bay Company that was formed before the west was even in Canada. There we found a lot of interesting things. There were not a lot of flowers but lots of creeping cedars on the hills. It was a lot of fun to slide down, but the most interesting thing we found was a bunch of old nests. They were about 4' across and made of twigs. We curled up in the nest and it fit 3 kids. I wondered what bird made it. Of course, we pictured a huge bird swooping down to carry us away, and we rode off pretty fast to get away from there. I had a very good imagination, so I could imagine those big birds swooping down to catch us as we galloped toward home.

When we weren't on the horse we still roamed the hills. We knew where to find the best crocuses and buttercups, larkspur, roses, sleeping johnnies, violets and more. We always had bouquets of flowers on the table for Mom.

A Welcome Rain Storm

Storm clouds blow across the sky
High above, the aeroplanes fly
The land is parched for lack of rain.
If this continues there will be no grain!

Pastures are brown, the pond's almost dry
"The gardens are planted," Mother says with a sigh.
The little seeds are nestled in the dry ground.
Not a drop of moisture could be found.

Bessie the cow calls a calf half her size
She's searching for grass, with very sad eyes.
Chickens are bathing in big pools of dust.
If we are to survive here, rain is a must.

Children are struggling and struggle they must
To walk in the dust storms of very fine dust.

Horses are walking a very slow gait.
Dirt is drifting by the garden gate.

Dogs are barking and beginning to complain
As they walk slowly down the long long lane.
No drop of rain came and very little snow
If God doesn't soon send some nothing will grow.

The farmer looks wistfully over the window sill
At the desolate brown field that was his to till.
Then his wife spoke softly, her eyes open wide,
"His promise is sure so the Lord will provide."

They looked up with wonder, they look to the west,
As the clouds grew darker o'er their family nest.
Then the children rush in and exclaim with delight
"Look father, look mother, it's raining tonight."

They stood there and watched as the rain found it's way
To the seeds and the grass and the much needed hay.
The horse was now prancing, the cow mooing low
Her calf was excited, and down the lane they did go.

The dogs quit their barking and rolled in delight
In the soft squishy mud, t'was quite a sight.
They stood there and watched then dropped to their knees,
Mother spoke gently, "Pray, Father, please."

So Father prayed softly as tears flowed down his face.
"Thank you, dear Father for your saving grace
And help us to remember all you have done
Help us to remember your beloved Son."

"Now help us to be thankful
For the blessings you bestow
And Help us to remember
The great love you do show"

They rose up slowly and lifted their heads
We have something to do before going to bed.
Take off your shoes, leave on your clothes
Let the mud squish up between your toes.

So out they all went in the rain that night
They played in the mud with all their might.
The rain came down quickly, but they didn't care,
For they were so thankful for God was up there.

The Garden

Evenings we would all go out to help Mom weed the garden, not willingly mind you. Those rows of vegetables that needed weeding seemed miles long. We would pick one weed and slap at two mosquitoes. The part of the garden I liked the best was the tomatoes.

In the spring before it quit freezing Mom used to build a hot house. The wooden walls were a couple feet high with windows on about a 45 degree slope for a roof. She dug a hole about a foot deep and put 6 inches of fresh horse manure in it, then topped it off with topsoil that had been removed. Then the seeds were planted and watered, and we closed the windows. The horse manure composted and gave off heat from below, and with the sun shining in the windows, it took no time at all before the plants began to grow. Once the danger of frost was over we planted the tomatoes and cabbage plants in the garden. By this time, they were big and healthy plants.

———

All August we picked peas and beans to can. We also had cucumbers for dill pickles and sometimes squash, tomatoes, cantaloupe and muskmelon. We didn't have a freezer, nor did we know you could eat them after they were frozen. When the cantaloupe was ready to pick Mom would put them, along with tomatoes, in boxes under the beds in the attic. This was a nice warm, dark place for them to ripen. In the fall, when we came home from school, we would rush upstairs, pull all the boxes out, and smell the cantaloupe. If one smelled sweet we'd rush down to the kitchen, slice it open, pour sugar on it, and munch away. It was such a treat.

———

One day in August Mom and we girls picked and shelled peas almost all day. Oh, what a hard job! Mom was finishing shelling the last few pods while we girls were starting to prepare supper before going to milk the cows. The men came in and headed for the sink to wash off some of the dirt that had attached itself to their face, arms and hands. Bud turned to Mom – "Well Mom what have you been doing all day?" That was what she usually asked them and was her way of saying, "Tell me how the work is coming along." She looked up and said, with a straight face, "Well, I've been peaing all day!" She had a rare sense of humour.

———

We ate a lot of peas, beans and corn fresh from the garden. We canned what was left. When Mom used to can fruit, vegetables or meat she put water in the boiler, put in the jars of fruit, set it on the cook stove, and boiled the water. When the time was up she lifted the jars out, tightened the lids and the process was done. Mom used to can carrots, peas, beans, dill pickles, beet pickles, fruit and even sauerkraut. She even pickled some eggs one time. We would carry the jars down to the basement and put them on shelves for use during the long winter.

———

With the cucumbers Mom made dill pickles. A meal wasn't a meal without dill pickles. She also made sauerkraut. She made it in crocks or sometimes in a wooden barrel. She kept it behind the house until it was ready to can. We used to sneak out, lift the rock and pieces of wood on top that kept the sauerkraut below the juice level, and stuck in a hand. We would bring out a fist full. It was oh-so-good. The juice would run down our arms and drip off of our elbows. What a mess! But we didn't care and my mouth still waters when I think of it.

———

Usually by the first of September it was already getting cold at night. Jars of dill pickles and beans and peas lined the shelves. Now it was almost freeze-up and it was potato harvest time. Daddy took the day off from wheat harvest, even if it wasn't done yet, and he announced we were taking a day off school to dig potatoes. The teacher didn't like it much, but since we were half the kids at school, and Daddy was on the school board, she kept her peace. As soon as morning chores were done, and breakfast was over, we piled into the lumber wagon and went to the garden, which was a half mile east of the house. Daddy followed with a team of horses and a plow. Daddy had the horse pull the plow down the row of potatoes, turning the soil and uncovering potatoes. We followed with buckets to gather the potatoes in. The soil was soft and cool under our feet as we walked along. It was very hard work and Daddy got upset if we didn't keep up. He couldn't dig another row until we picked up this one. So, all day long 8 little legs ran as fast as they could. We filled bucket after bucket with potatoes and ran to the big wagon, dumped them in and ran to fill the buckets again. Before we finished, the sun was getting low in the sky and it was getting really cold. While we gathered potatoes Mom and one of the younger ones would search the cucumber vines for any cucumbers that were left. They also went over the corn patch for a few more of the cobs left that they could harvest and dug the few turnips and carrots that were still in the ground. The wagon was usually full by the time we were done. I remember one time we didn't take notice of where we parked the wagon. We thought that it would be a good idea to put the wagon closer to the garden so that we didn't have to walk all the way to the road. We put it in the edge of the garden in soft soil. By the time we got the wagon loaded Daddy had already gone the ½ mile back to the house with the team of horses. We all climbed on the wagon that was heaped as full as it could be. The wagon wheels had sunk into the soft soil because the wagon was so heavy. The poor old faithful mules tried to pull it. They pulled and pulled. When we saw how hard they were pulling we all jumped off for fear they would break their backs. They still couldn't pull the wagon. We unhitched them, walked them home. Daddy brought a team of big horses to pull the wagon to the house. Now it was getting dark and frost in the air. We had to hurry to get the vegetables into the basement before they froze. Daddy had built a big bin in the basement about 6 x 10 feet square and right to the ceiling. He opened the little window, on the side of the basement, rigged up a chute and poured the potatoes down into the bin. They filled the bin to the rafters. The rest of the vegetables we carried in buckets down the basement stairs and put in a separate bin. The next day we rigged up boxes of sand and buried the carrots in sand to keep them fresh. They usually stayed quite nice until close to Christmas.

Tobogganing

We loved it when the men hooked up the horses to the sleigh with the hayrack on it. We would tie our toboggan on behind and go for a ride. Perhaps I should describe our toboggan. One day Daddy came home with an old discarded metal sign – about 2' by 5'. "It is very heavy," he said, "therefore very strong". He bent the one end a little bit, nailed a 2" by 4" board on each side, attached a rope to the front and wow! – we had a toboggan! We were thrilled! It was so heavy that we needed 2 or 3 of us to pull it up a hill. When the snow was soft it was too heavy and wouldn't work because it would sink in the soft snow, but when the snow was hard packed or drifted we had some great rides.

A few years later Daddy came home from town with a brand-new wooden toboggan. It seemed light as a feather and long enough for four of us to ride at once. Now we could head for bigger hills. It was so easy to pull up the hills. I wish I knew how many miles that toboggan went. The wood started to get thin from its many trips down the hill.

Now we had two toboggans to tie behind the hayrack. The boys used to run the horses as fast as they could to give us an exciting ride as they headed for the stack yard for hay. They tried to dump us off if they could as we bounced in and out of the ruts in the snow that were made by the sleigh and the horses' hooves. Usually we had snow up our sleeves, down our neck and our faces covered. It was pretty cold, but oh so much fun! The ride back from the stack yard was much slower. The load was heavy and would have been a big cleanup job if they tipped it over, so the guys were pretty careful on the ride back.

More Chores

When 3 p.m. came, it was time to get the lamps

ready to light since we didn't have electricity. Darkness seemed to creep up on you and it was best to get this done well before you needed to have a light. We gathered the lamps together. All the coal oil lamps needed filling and the globes cleaned. If we didn't clean the soot off them, we didn't get a very bright light. We also had to trim the wicks. It was a tedious job but not too bad. In the fall there were always a lot of miller moths fluttering around the lights. We had fun catching them in our hands, and holding them over the lamp globe until the moths dropped in. They fluttered a while, but they were soon dead. Then we would catch another moth and do it again. From time to time we had to lift the globe and dump the dead moths out there were so many.

Coal oil lamps didn't give a very good light but that was all we had for a long time. I well remember when Daddy came home with our first gas lamp. It was all so new. He put gas into it then he tied a mantle on and put a match up to it. I thought, "That was a mistake. It all burnt up". But I didn't understand that it was supposed to. The ash stayed on and that was how the lamp gave its light. This lamp was a miracle. It gave a really bright light. Daddy hung it on a hook that was put in the center of the ceiling of the room. Now we could see to read or do our

embroidery anywhere we wanted to sit instead of having to sit close to a coal oil lamp. It was much easier to do our chores of dishes or milk separating when we could see so well too. This was Classy living.

————

Since we didn't have indoor plumbing, the chamber pots also had to be emptied. We carried them to the hill behind the house and dumped them. We hurried back to get away from the smell. Oh, what a yucky job! Once they were emptied, Mom usually spared us the job of cleaning and disinfecting them - we were very glad for her to do that job and cleaning them sure helped the smell.

Milking

By dusk we had to get the cows in to milk. Usually they were waiting by the door eager to get into the barn. So, we lit the old coal oil lantern, put on our barn clothes – which were overalls, an old coat and a white kerchief on our heads - which were really worn out diapers and tuck it in on each side of our face. It made us look like nuns. We were very careful to tie it on to cover our hair so that we didn't get to smell like a cow since we leaned on her while we milked. We had a lot of cats which loved to squat nearby while we milked. As we milked we would squirt milk across the barn into their mouths. The cows ate their hay contentedly while we milked. As we were milking we got to thinking a bit of what it must have been like when our Lord Jesus was born – like when we sing "Away In A Manger" and where it says "the cattle are lowing." It also helped to pass the time. With milking done, we were ready for supper.

––––––––––

One winter, Daddy said, "Milking cows is not a ladies' job, you should stay in and help your mother in the house. The boys can milk the cows." That was good news! We busied ourselves helping mom make meals and clean house and all of the other chores mother had to do every day.

A week later mother said, "I don't know what has happened to the cows, but we hardly have enough milk to drink, and not nearly enough cream to ship". The boys finally admitted that they weren't milking the cows dry. They only partly milked them. The cows did what nature tells them, "We don't need so much milk, so quite making so much." "Well" daddy said, "girls! go back to the barn and milk again." It took us over a week of milking the cows to get the production back to where it was before the boys had taken over. From then on, we had to do all the milking. The guys thought it funny and leisurely forked hay and did the few chores they needed to do while we milked. They didn't want to be done before we were finished milking. That would have shown Daddy that we did more work than they did.

––––––––––

After supper while some were doing dishes, someone would put the milk through the milk separator to separate the cream from the milk. The cream was stored in the cupboard to be shipped once a week to Moose Jaw. There it would be made into butter. In the winter, the milk was cooled in the snow bank for the family's use. The men never did much in the evening. Sometimes they brought in wood but usually Earl and George did that. We girls did that as well as all of the milking, washing dishes, baking, helping in the kitchen, feeding the chickens and other chores.

(photo: this is the lower barn by the creek where we milked cows and kept the horses and a few pigs)

Stories

Sometimes Daddy would tell us stories after supper while he drank his tea. For a while they were about "Hop on my Thumb," who was a small boy the size of a thumb. In his adventures he rode on a robin. He rode on its back and landed on a windowsill. Hop on my Thumb had close calls with cats and other exciting adventures. When Daddy got to a spot where he needed time to think of what would happen next, he would say "Just a minute, I need some tea". Then he would take his time to slowly pour tea and fix it just right with cream. He then would take a long sip before he continued. It wasn't long before we heard those dreaded words – "Well that's all for tonight." We came abruptly back to reality and had to get back to our chores.

The long evening together was so nice. Sometimes we all played games, but often the girls did embroidery while the boys played games. Daddy usually read his book.

Radio Arrives

One day when I was about 7, Daddy came home from the city with a fancy little box. "This is a radio", daddy told us. "What is a radio? I ask. "Well in Regina" daddy explained, "they have a broadcasting station, it sends signals into the air. This radio picks the signals up and plays them for us." When it was all set up, Daddy turned a knob on the front and singing and talking came out. This was my introduction to the radio. Irene told me that there were little people inside. "Really! I stuck a pin in through the speaker and someone said, 'Ouch! Someone stuck me with a pin!'" I looked and couldn't see them, but she said, "They were so small you couldn't see them". For a long time, I imagined what they looked like. I made sure the radio didn't get too close to the edge of the shelf, so the little people didn't fall off.

The radio was the center of interest on long winter evenings. We hurried with chores and supper dishes so that we could gather around and listen to Lux Radio Theatre, Henry Aldrich, My Friend Irma, The Shadow and many more programs. We also got weather reports and news.

———

Often if there was a storm at sea Daddy would call upstairs long into the night with updates on ships that were in trouble and I went to sleep praying for them.

———

Superman show always came on about 5:30 so I hurried and did my cow milking and feeding of chickens so I was done in time to listen. I'm sure Mom was thankful many times for Superman. She never had to bug me to work as long as he was on. I was in love with superman.

After School Activities

When we arrived home from school we always had a snack. Often Mom had freshly baked bread. It really bugged Mom though when she had fresh bread on the table and we cut all the crusts off and left just the soggy centre. We didn't get away with that often, but when we did, we still had to suffer the consequences and eat the soggy centre for supper. We all liked the crust the best.

Sometimes we would haul out the old cast iron fry pan and make popcorn. Of course, we always had a lot of butter to pour on it. What a treat! The aroma filled the house.

Once in a while we would have a toffee pull. Once the toffee mixture was about finished boiling, we brought in a piece of ice. A small amount was dropped onto the ice and if it hardened the toffee was ready to be pulled. We then loaded our hands with butter and started to pull. Hazel would say, "Keep pulling until it turns almost white". Trouble was by that time it really turned to grey. I guess our hands were not very clean – so when we realized why this happened it all went in the garbage. Oh well, it was fun anyway. By that time we had butter dripping off of our elbows because as we pulled it, it became more sticky so we kept adding butter to our hands. We had nibbled along the way and really didn't want to eat anymore anyway because it was so sweet, so weren't too disappointed to throw it out. We had had the fun of pulling it.

————

The long winter nights were great. After dishes and chores were all done it was time to relax. The games came out. One year, Daddy had gotten us a table croquet set. We spread a blanket on the big kitchen table and wire wickets stuck through the blanket and the challenge was on. With little wooden mallets and little wooden balls, it made for an evening of fun. Many an hour we spent going around and around the table, hitting those little balls and trying to get them through the wickets. Another year we got a Monopoly set. Hours and hours were spent buying and selling property. While we were playing games, Mom either played checkers with the little ones, or sat mending socks or knitting mittens. Sometimes, we gathered around the potbelly stove in the living room. Often, we girls did embroidery and the boys played board games or just talked.

Mishaps and the doctor

One night, Earl and I were restless. We decided to play "bucking horse". One of us would stand in the chair hanging on to the back. The other would crawl under it, arch our back and make the chair bounce like a real bucking horse. We had both had several turns when I decided to give Earl a special ride just like a real horse. I arched my back and gave a mighty buck. The chair tipped over and Earl's hands, which were hanging on to the back of the chair, fell against the red-hot heater. Oh, I felt so bad! Earl screamed and screamed. The kids all bawled me out and I guess I should have thought it could happen. I was just trying to do something fun for my little brother.

———

Earl, George and Linda all had convulsions when they were little. They went away as they got older but it sure was scary. One time, George had a really bad convulsion. Evelyn asked the doctor, "What should we do?" He replied, "We really don't know, but I think that you should put his feet in warm water when it happens. Then put cold cloths on his forehead." Sure enough, it wasn't long before George had another spell. There was a dish of warm water on the stove, so someone grabbed the dish and shoved his feet in, shoes and all. They didn't want to waste time to take his shoes off. Someone grabbed a towel, dipped it in cold water and put it on his head. Soon he recovered and started to scream. No one knew why until they took his shoes off. He had bad burns on his feet which later turned into huge blisters. I guess the water was hotter than we realized, and the shoes held the heat in. He had to see the Doctor a lot and finally had to have the blisters lanced to get them to heal.

The night the doctor came to lance the blisters we had just made ice cream, and neighbours had come down to help us eat it. As the doctor and Evelyn went to the living room to work on George's feet we all started to chant – "I scream, you scream, we all scream for ice cream." We were told to wait until the doctor left and to be quiet. Well, we just continued to chant though, in a stage whisper for half an hour until the doctor left.

I still don't know why it was bad for us to eat ice cream when the Dr. was there, and I am sure it would have been a lot more appropriate for us to be able to eat the ice cream to keep us quiet, but the neighbour lady thought she was doing the right thing. George's feet soon healed, and he was able to walk again and even put on his shoes.

The Flat Barn and The Sheep Barn

Across the yard from the house we had a big flat roof barn. We called it the muck barn because it was never cleaned out all winter and the roof leaked. By spring you couldn't walk in it without sinking in muck. During the summer the men used to clean it out to make it ready for shelter for the cattle come winter. They used to stack a lot of oat sheaves on top in the fall to make it easy to throw feed down to the cattle. The straw and sheaves that were left by spring gave the mice a great place to nest. All summer we used to scale the walls. It was so much fun. Once we mastered one side we tried the next side. Finding a toehold here and a finger hold there. It was very rewarding to reach the top. Sometimes if we moved a sheaf we would find a mouse nest. The babies were so cute and very tiny. For fun we would get a matchbox, pack it with cotton batten or wool to make a bed and fill it with babies and wrap it up as a gift and give it to Evelyn. When she opened it, she would scream, and the box went flying. After a good laugh, we would go back and play. She was such a good sport! We knew how she hated mice.

Beside the muck barn was a high peaked barn we called the sheep barn. It too was just a shelter made of 6-inch wide board sides and roof. There were no shingles. The sheep only needed a place to get in out of the snow. We often had a couple hundred sheep. The little lambs started coming in January. A lot of the times we had a lamb or two in a cardboard box sitting on our oven door. Sometimes Daddy would come stumbling in from the bitter cold all covered with snow carrying a tiny bundle. Sometimes he would have two. Often, we thought they were dead because they were so stiff. Mom would put them on the warm oven door and take a soft cloth and rub them down really well. Soon the eyelids would open, and it would lift its little head up. Mom took a pop bottle with a nipple and gave them a drink of warm milk. Usually by morning they were ready to go out to mamma and nurse.

One summer day the men were all sitting in the kitchen having coffee and Daddy said he wanted to tear the big sheep barn down but didn't know when he would find time. He seemed quite upset but he didn't seem to be in a hurry to get back to work either. I could have told him how he could find time – just skip reading mystery stories in the daytime – but I didn't. Instead, we girls offered to do it. At first, he said, "No." Then he said,

"Go ahead." He didn't think that we could or that we even knew how. By the time the men got back to work, we already had a bunch of boards off the roof. Well, we had been climbing like monkeys all over it for a long time so being on top was no big deal. In a few days we had all the boards off and were trying to figure out how we could get the trusses down when Mom stepped in and told Dad we had done well, but if we tried to climb the trusses to take them down we would get hurt. The men then took over. Really, it was work but it was a lot of fun too. And Daddy was surprised to find that he had such capable girls.

Bath Night

I well remember bath night as a little girl. Mom would bring in the boiler. It was a large oval shaped pan 2½ feet long, 1 foot wide and 16 inches deep. She used this when she did her canning. She also sometimes used it on wash day. She would put soapy water in it, fill it with clothes and put it on the stove to heat. After the clothes soaked in the hot soapy water, they came clean in the washing machine. We often admired her white clothes as they reflected the sun while they

fluttered in the wind on the lines.

Bath night Mom would stoke the cook stove and fill the boiler with water. In the wintertime we brought in ice from the creek to fill the boiler. After supper we brought in the old tin bathtub. In the winter it was all covered with frost, but Mom put it in front of the stove with the oven door open and to warm it up. Baths always started with the youngest child. Mom would put an inch of water in the tub and bathe the baby. When the next youngest was ready, another dipper of hot water was added. The children were first, ladies next and the men last. After we were bathed, all of us girls would sit around the big kitchen table curling our hair. We propped up mirrors on the table and sometimes we'd do each other's hair. Evelyn, my oldest sister, was my favourite. She was like a second mother to me. She liked to fuss over me, and sometimes she would curl our

hair in rag curlers. She tore strips of rags from an old worn out sheet, 1½ inches by 8 inches. If she wanted ringlets, she wound the hair round and round, then wind the rag around the hair and tied the two ends together. If she wanted just curls she wound the hair the shape of a curl and tied the rag ends. When she was finished I looked like Toppsie, the little black girl in the newspaper ads. The rag curlers worked quite well. When we got older we did our hair in what we called pin curls - using bobby pins instead of the rags. Sometimes we would try to fancy Mom up and curl the sides of her hair. She was so beautiful and always wore her hair pulled straight back, and in a bun, but she liked it when we curled the sides.

––––––––

Every year Mom bought yards and yards of white flannelette. She used it to make diapers for the latest baby – but she also used it to make nightgowns for us. She folded the flannelette in half and made a neck hole for our heads to go through. Then she made straight sleeves for our arms. The gowns were always floor length and warm. When we got new gowns, we felt like we were real live princesses. The soft white, fluffy gowns were so special! They were always floor length, so we could tuck our feet in the soft folds and it felt so good. Of course, since I was so small, I had more to tuck my feet in to.

––––––––

One winter bath night was very funny, but scary at the same time. The men were not home. They had gone to town and had not yet returned. We younger ones were done with our baths. Mom and my older sister were ready to get undressed and have our baths when we saw lights coming down the lane. We ran to peek out the window and saw a couple of Norwegian neighbours – Gus and Daniel. They were driving a tractor and were very drunk. They stumbled to the house and came in. Most of us hid in the living room and peeked through the crack in the door. I don't know if they saw 6 or 7 pairs of eyes in the crack or not.

Mom humoured them and asked what they wanted. "We want to talk politics with Jim," they said. Mom told them Jim wasn't home and she finally talked them into leaving. She said, "Go home to your wives. Leave the bottle here and don't drink anymore." After falling off the tractor a couple of times they left. We watched their taillights until they turned the corner heading home. That was a lot of excitement for one night. Mom said, "Their poor wives, I feel sorry for them."

Sometimes when we couldn't bring in the big tub, Mom would put a round washtub in the living room close to the potbelly stove. There we could wash and stand near the stove to keep warm while we dried.

Storms

Winter storms were sometimes very bad. It was easy to lose your way and get lost in the storm. Mom always kept a light in the window just in case someone was lost. "It would guide them to safety." she would say.

About 3:30 p.m. one stormy day, Mom said, "Girls, I need some drinking water before dark." Hazel and Irene bundled up, grabbed two buckets and headed outside. It was a long trudge through the snow, across the yard and down the hill to the well. Mom waited and waited for them to return. It would soon be dark, and the girls were not back yet. We lit the lamps and trimmed the wicks so that the lamps would burn their brightest. It was so cozy in the house with the lamps burning, but the wind was whistling outside.

Still the girls didn't come back. By the time we were finished lighting the lamps, Mom was wringing her hands and pacing the floor with worry. Hazel and Irene must have gotten lost. We pictured finding them in the morning frozen to death in a snowbank. Daddy headed for his coat and began to bundle up and pull on his boots. "Where are you going?" cried Mom. "I'm going out to get my girls," Daddy calmly replied. "My girls are out there, and I will find them!" "If I lose two girls it would be awful, but if I lost you too I couldn't bear it," Mom cried. "Don't worry," comforted Daddy, "I know this place like the back of my hand. I will bring the girls back."

So, Daddy went out and we all prayed. Half an hour later when it was almost black out and the storm was still raging, we heard a noise at the door. I ran to open it. In stumbled Hazel, Irene and Daddy all covered with snow. We rushed to close the door behind them to keep out the storm. "We had trouble breaking the ice in the well," explained Hazel, "We finally broke through and here is the water."

Walking Home in a Storm

We almost always had the mules to take us to school, but a few times we had to walk the 3½ miles across country. One time, as we were walking home, it started to hail very hard. There was no shelter and the hail hurt so bad. We put our dinner pails (we used Rogers Syrup cans or jam cans) on our head. That protected our head, but we got very bruised fingers.

Another time it started to storm and snow. The neighbours came to school and got their kids. Since the teacher lived near them she sent us home on foot, so she could leave too. We barely got started when the storm closed in. We had no fences or a road to follow, just a track in the snow, which was soon covered. What could we do? We lined up in a row – following the leader. Irene lead, Hazel was last. I was in the middle to keep track of Earl, my little brother. Irene headed for home and kept calling, "You OK?" I called, "You OK?" Earl called "You OK?" then Hazel called "I'm OK!" and so on until Irene heard all were OK. We prayed all the way home, "Lord help us get home safely."

Every few minutes we would do this. When Irene couldn't face the snow anymore, she traded places with Hazel. We finally got home, very cold, but we got there safely. We almost got lost, because we were ½ mile off track. It is a good thing we did lots of wandering the hills and knew the shape of the hills. because that is what lead us home. It was a foolish thing for the teacher to do to send four young children off across country in a snow storm. We could have easily been lost and could all have been frozen to death, but the Lord graciously got us safely home. Daddy was so mad. The teacher nearly lost her job. Daddy said that he could easily have lost all four of us.

Storm-stayed overnight

It was a snowy day in January. Uncle Dewey was our teacher, I was in grade nine. Uncle Dewey was busy trying to pound some knowledge into our heads. He got very frustrated with us at times. He was so smart, and he knew the work so well that he couldn't understand why we didn't do better at understanding what he taught us.

This day he was a bit more nervous. He kept glancing out the window. I kept thinking, "What is so interesting outside?" We soon found out. There was a storm coming and we better hurry home. We closed our books and headed for our coats. The older kids headed out to the barn to get the mules hooked up to the sleighs. The rest of the kids gathered up the books and dinner pails.

Within a few minutes the storm hit with a vengeance. Snow was coming down thick and heavy. The wind grew even stronger. Uncle Dewey said, "We'll have to stay, it will soon be dark, and we will get lost. We couldn't even make it if it were daylight. Look! We can't even see the barn, or the horses and sleighs." as he headed out to tell the kids to put the horses back into the barn.

I have no doubt that we would have been ok because our faithful mules would have taken us home safely. The other kids however were not so fortunate. Their horses were really quite dumb.

"We'll stay the night. Perhaps it will clear by morning." Uncle Dewey told us as he went to the basement to stoke the stove and set out more coal to feed the fire during the night. "We have no light, so it needs to be close, so we can find it once it gets dark", he explained.

"Good," I thought, "He isn't going to ask me to stoke the fire." I was relieved, I was terribly afraid of the dark. The basement had cement walls but only a uneven dirt floor. Cobwebs hung everywhere. The two windows were very tiny so even in the day time it was dark and dingy and scary. I imagined all kinds of spooky creatures coming after me from under the steps or around the corner of the coal bin or from behind the furnace. When it was dark it was even more scary. The fire crackled and sparked. The cold, freezing weather made the school house make loud noises as the frost drove the cold deep into the walls. It sounded like a gun was being shot. The basement was not a place I wanted to be.

This was the worst storm that had hit the country for years. The wind was whistling in the windows, making little piles of snow on the window sills, everywhere there was a tiny crack.

The night seemed endless. We were hungry, and the night had not begun yet. Out came the dinner pails. We shared what was left of our lunch. Those few crusts of bread tasted so good.

Hazel, my older sister wasn't satisfied, "I'll make some biscuits," she announced. "We have flour and water." The flour and water was what we used to make paste (or glue) for art work.

She mixed flour and water and made biscuits. Our mouths watered at the thought as she put her freshly made biscuits on a lunch pail lid and put it on the register to cook. Half an hour later she declared them done and let us try them. Ugh! They were totally inedible. She was so disappointed and so were we.

"Go to sleep," Uncle Dewey announced, "Time will go by faster." So, we gathered all the blankets and coats we could find and spread them around the floor register. Sleep would not come. The floor was too hard, the kids closest to the register got too hot, those not so close thought they would freeze. We could feel the wind as it crept through the cracks in the windows and doors.

Then someone had to go to the bathroom. Since the toilet was outside connected to the barn, we decided to all go at the same time. We all put on our coats and boots and headed out side. We held hands and went in a long line, praying we would not get lost. Darkness was beginning to set in. The girls' toilet was on the east side of the barn, and the boys' was on the west. Each toilet had two holes with a wooden box under the holes. In the summertime the boxes were removed and dumped. In the meantime, it got very smelly.

Once we got back into the school we tried to sleep. Sleep avoided us like the plague. I think this was the longest night I have ever spent.

Eventually it began to get light out. Cheers went up. The storm had stopped. Once again, the teams were hitched to the sleighs, dinner pails gathered up and we headed home. The storm had cleared but it was bitterly cold. I think it was about -30 degrees but there was no wind. Frost crystals were in the air and sparkled in the sun like a million diamonds floating around. We were shocked to see the huge snow drifts we had to plunge through to get home.

Our parents were excited to get us home. They had worried all night fearing that we were lost in the storm.

Coffee was brewed, and we ate a record amount of breakfast. We were tired but so thankful the Lord had brought us safely home.

Spring Flood/Rush home from school

We used to have lots of snow. In Saskatchewan spring comes suddenly. We had to cross the creek to get to school. As long as the snow melted slowly we were okay, but every spring the creek flooded high in a few hours once the water started to flow. As ice started to break up, ice jams formed upstream. When they began to break the creek turned into a mighty torrent.

It was spring, and water was running everywhere. The huge snow banks were shriveling up like a tired old man. Excitement was in the air. Spring was always an exciting time.

Little lambs and little calves were making their entrance into the world. They would run around kicking up their heels while they played. Their mothers stayed close by keeping a watchful eye for fear the dogs may try to bother them. I used to imagine them saying, "I'm so glad to be alive." Soon the trees and flowers would burst into life too, buds on the trees were already swelling.

Mom kept an eye on the creek for signs of rising water. When it showed signs of overflowing the banks

Daddy jumped on old Nelly and rode as fast as he could to come and get us.

At school Irene was sharpening her pencil at the sharpener that was fastened to the wall near the window. I was always amazed at how often the big kids had to sharpen their pencils. I hadn't yet learned that this was a convenient way to be able to look out of the window without getting into trouble. Suddenly she whispered, "Daddy's coming." It was only 2 o'clock. "The horse is at full gallop."

"Why was he coming? It's only 2 o'clock", I thought.

Daddy burst into the room, he threw us a pillow case and said, "Put some books in these but hurry." We knew it would be at least a week before we would be able to cross the creek to come back to school. So, we piled books into the pillow cases, not that we would look at them, but it was what the teacher wanted us to do. We grabbed our coats and boots and wriggled into them as we ran for the wagon.

Irene rode the horse back home while Daddy drove the mules with our wagon. It was a rude awakening for poor old Jack and Jenny. We always let them go as slow as they wanted, but now out came the whip and they had to go as fast as they could. We had two and a half miles to go to cross the creek. It was a race between them and the flood. They must win, or we would be at least a week before we could go home.

When we got to the creek I was bewildered! Wow, what had happened to the creek? This morning it was running but not very much and we had easily crossed. Now it was a mighty rushing torrent and the banks were nowhere to be seen. We couldn't even tell where the crossing was.

Daddy said, "It's rising fast. If we don't make it in the next few minutes, we won't get across. I think the crossing is about here, so I'll try here." The faithful old mules waded into the water, deeper and deeper and soon they were swimming. The wagon box began to fill with water. "Stand the book bag on the dinner pails," Hazel yelled. Now the wagon box began to float, it looked like it might float downstream. "Please Lord, help us get across," I prayed.

There were four posts rising from the wagon frame. These kept the box in place. "Hang onto the wagon posts!" someone yelled. The water got deeper and deeper. The mules were swimming hard battling against the mighty current of the rushing water.

The wagon box had floated almost to the top of the posts, but still we hung on for dear life. We hung on so tightly that our knuckles were white. One more inch to go and it would have floated above the posts and our little hands were not strong enough to stop it from floating away. I looked across at the swirling water and wondered if the box would tip over and dump us all out into the creek. Then it happened! The mules' feet touched solid ground. They had been swept a long way down stream, but now they touched solid ground and they slowly pulled the wagon up and out of the creek.

What a relief! Water ran out of the wagon. The mules even looked relieved. The faithful old mules came through a tough spot again. It was a short distance to the barn. We all piled out. "Look" Daddy said. "we did it. It is unbelievable! If we had been five minutes later, we never could have made it." A surge of water had come down the creek and it was a very angry, roaring river.

We were off school for a week or more until the flood went down. We could play outside all we wanted and didn't even have to play sick to get time off school. It was so much fun to help the streams in the yard as they made a mighty dash to join their brothers in the mighty rush down to the creek.

Ice Box Arrives

We never had electricity; therefore, we never had a refrigerator. So, when Grandma Schobert died, Mom brought home her icebox. An icebox is a wooden cupboard. The top lifts up, and you put a block of ice in. Below there are doors that opened to a compartment for food (*see photo*).   As the ice melts it cools the food compartment. It was so nice to have cool milk to drink.

———————

One time, we girls got fancy and made a layer cake and iced it really nicely. We only ate about 1/3 of it so into the icebox it went. The next day, after supper, we went to the icebox to get the cake for dessert. Did we get a shock when we saw it! The icing was all there but there was no cake! Earl finally confessed that he had gotten a spoon and dug it all out and ate it. For some reason he never even got in trouble for it. Earl never seemed to get into trouble for things he did.

———————

You may ask, "How did you keep the milk cool before you had an ice box?" It was hard. We put it in syrup pails or jars and put them on the cool basement floor. The milk had a tendency to sour quickly, so Mom always kept a crock of milk on the back of the stove, keeping warm to make it into cottage cheese. That way the milk didn't go to waste. After a day or so, when it was almost ready, we used to dip in and get a dish of curds. With salt and pepper - it was so good! My mouth waters thinking about it. In the winter we put the milk cans in a snow bank and kept the milk cold that way. At mealtime we brought it in and scraped the ice crystals off the sides. Oh, it was so good.

We never usually cooled the cream, except for a bit to whip or for coffee. It went sour, but once a week we put it all in a 5-gallon cream can and the train took it to a Moose Jaw dairy for butter making.

Where did we get the ice for the ice box?

A soon as the ice was thick enough to drive on in the fall, the men used to get ice from the creek for water for Mom to wash clothes in. It was very soft water and the clothes were very soft and white when mom used the ice for washing.

To get ice for the ice box, the men took a pick and chipped holes in the ice, then they used shovels to put the ice chips in barrels which were placed on a stone boat and then pulled up in front of the house.

A stone boat was a kind of sleigh made with two 4 X 4's and topped with planks. The stone boat was pulled in the fields and loaded with stones during other times of year. Stones could cause a big problem with the farm machinery. The stones were then hauled off and put in a stone pile. The stone boat was also used to load manure when we cleaned the barn. They then pulled it to a field and spread it out to work into the soil in the spring.

In the winter, however, the stone boat was used to haul these barrels of ice to melt for baths, washing clothes, and scrubbing floors. When Mom said, "Girls, I need water." we grabbed some pails and filled the boiler with ice. The boiler was placed on the old cook stove, and we waited for the ice to melt.

One fall, Daddy dug a hole like a basement and put a granary on it. The hole was lined with rocks to keep it from caving in. We called this the ice house. When the ice, on the creek, was about one foot thick the men took an ice saw and cut squares of ice, pulled them out with ice tongs and stored the blocks in the icehouse. Once the hole was full, they covered it with a couple feet of straw. The straw insulated the ice, so it stayed frozen most of the summer. We used to love to go there and crawl on the rafters. If we fell, we had a soft landing. That is, until a lot of the ice was gone by late summer. I have a few big scars on my head to show for some of my falls. I hated to get the ice – the place was dark, wet, moldy and had mice which I really hated.

Making Ice Cream

We all loved ice cream. Since we had lots of milk we could make ice cream whenever we wanted, as long as ice was available. While one of us was mixing the milk and cream to make ice cream, someone else prepared the ice. We took a bunch of chunks of ice and put them into a potato sack. We then fastened the top

shut, took a hammer and smashed the ice into very small pieces. This wasn't a bad job in the winter when we could go to the ice barrel and get the ice or even go to the creek and chip it from the frozen creek. But in the summer, we had to go down into the moldy, wet straw in the icehouse. That was an awful job.

The ice cream maker consisted of a small wooden barrel with a metal container inside, about a gallon in size. Inside this was a set of metal paddles that turned and scraped the frozen ice cream off the sides. Once we had the ice ready and ice cream mixture ready we could start the job of making ice cream. The milk mixture was poured into the metal tub, the beaters put in place and the lid carefully put on. Then we set this tub into the wooden barrel, fastened the crank top across it and secured the clasp in place. Then we slowly turned the crank. We took handfuls of ice and sprinkled it around the metal tub. We put a few inches of ice then sprinkled a bit of salt, more ice, more salt until the ice came almost to the top of the tub. As the salt made the ice melt it drove the frost inward and made the ice cream begin to form. As the ice melted water formed. There was a drain hole in the side of the wooden barrel to drain excess water. If the hole got plugged, then water rose, and salt water got into the ice cream. So, we kept watch and moved ice pieces away from the drain. Salty ice cream does not taste good! We had to keep the handle turning so it kept the sides scraped or it would freeze before all the liquid was turned to ice cream. Sometimes it only took a short while to make the ice cream, other times it took ever so long. It likely depended on the temperature that the milk and cream started out when it was put into the ice cream freezer. When the ice cream was ready to serve Daddy liked to pull the paddles out, put them on a plate with all the ice cream that stuck to it. This was his. The rest was ours. Then we all got our bowls filled. It was so good!

Sewing machine arrives

One day a man arrived with a treadle sewing machine. It was so shiny and new. Since we had no electricity, we had to power the sewing machine by hand, or perhaps I should say by foot. As long as we kept our feet pedaling, the machine sewed. It wasn't long before we got so used to pedaling, that we never had to think about it, but could think about what we were working on instead.

You should see how fast it could sew! The patches on clothes, that took Mom all night to sew before, she could do in a few minutes. She didn't get sore fingers from pushing the needle through the heavy material of Daddy's overalls either. When she wasn't using the sewing machine, we used to try to sew tents and doll clothes out of old sheets. I used to dream of being a seamstress one day. My big sister, Evelyn, sewed dresses for me. I must have been her favourite because she sewed for me, curled my hair and best of all we were bed pals. We used to cuddle up together to sleep. She was the best big sister I could have ever asked for.

Winter Clothes

We never had very warm clothes. Often, we put on two coats and 2 or 3 pair of mittens. Some of our mitts were knit, but mostly Mom just knit mitts for Daddy. She used to make mitts for the rest of us out of worn out socks. She would cut the feet off the sock and sew the end shut. Then make a thumb on the side to sew on. They were nice and long and came well up our little arms to keep the snow out.

Our boots were called overshoes because they went over your shoes. They were not warm like kids have today. They were like boot type tennis shoes, made of canvas with a rubber sole and with buckles to close them instead of shoe strings. So, so cold and took about 30 seconds for the cold to go through them when we wore them outside. I almost never left the yard on the way to school without crying because my feet were so cold already. Mom tried to heat rocks to put in the straw in the sleigh, but it didn't help much. We used to stomp our feet, run on the spot, anything to keep circulation so they wouldn't freeze. When they hurt you knew they were okay. When they stopped hurting you knew they were freezing, and you were in for trouble. Once your toes freeze, you don't feel them. That is until they warm up. Then, boy oh boy, do they hurt!

A lot of our clothes were hand-me-downs. We used to get boxes from our cousins in the city. Not much was wearable, but we used what we could. What was unusable, Mom and Evelyn unpicked the seams and remade them. One time, Daddy came back from Regina with a bunch of boxes. We had so much fun trying on clothes and laughing at some of the ridiculous stuff that was sent. Then in the bottom of the box were some skates! Out of the four pair we found one pair that we could manage to use. They were dull as could be and the eyelets for laces half pulled out. The blades were also loose, from the sole, but we spent many a happy time at the creek trying to learn to skate. The skates were too big, so we just had to keep putting socks on until they were tight enough to fit a little bit better. I think I had four pair of socks on and still they didn't work. So, I never learned to skate, but it was nearly impossible to skate on them anyway. Half the rivets had broken loose, so they didn't lace up very well, and the blades flopped back and forth when you tried to move.

(in photo L-R – Linda, George, and Shirley in front of the wagon that we went to school in)

Our Christmas at Home

In August the catalogues arrived. Since all our shopping was done by catalogue, we spent weeks pouring over them. There were so many clothes and toys. We knew we wouldn't get many toys, but it was fun to dream. If we needed shoes, Mom traced our feet on paper – cut it out and mailed it in. They sent the size we needed. It was a big job to clothe nine kids. Every fall we always needed boots and mitts. As we grew, our coats were handed down to the younger ones. Our boots were always totally worn out by the end of the season, so we needed new ones and couldn't pass them along.

My Sharon Marie

The toy section in the catalogue was what fascinated us most. We knew we didn't stand a hope of getting many toys but, hey, we could dream. I remember when Barbara Ann Scott won at the Olympics in figure skating. They had a Barbara Ann doll in the catalogue – skates and ruffled outfit and all. I had no idea of what figure skating was. I hadn't ever seen anyone even skate – except my sisters trying on the broken skates we were given, but that doll was so cute. I just needed one, but of course, I never got one. They were just too expensive.

I only ever had two dolls. One was a baby wet'm doll. She had a rubber tube from her mouth to her bottom. You fed her a bottle and it ran right through. Great idea but she was made out of sawdust and glue (called composition) and she disintegrated when she got wet a lot. Then, when I was about seven I got another doll with composition head, hands and feet and cloth body. Oh, how I loved her! I called her Sharon Marie. I always said when I had a little girl I would call her that. She had little shoes and white socks. Her dress was light pink organdie and she had a bonnet with a brim which I kept starched and ironed so it would stand up nicely. Many a night I went to sleep hugging her.

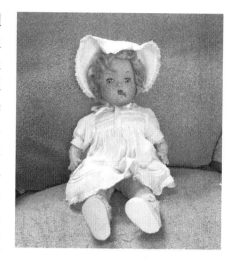

After I was grown and away, living in the city for a couple of years, I went home to get her. Mom had just painted her and given her to a missionary. I was broken-hearted. I would have willingly bought a new one for the missionary. A few years ago, I found one exactly like her in an antique store. Dress, shoes and all. When I hugged her and shut my eyes the memories came flooding back. I had my Sharon Marie back at last!

Christmas Eve

When Evelyn was home, she usually cleaned the living room the day before Christmas, but this one time she went in there mid-afternoon and shut the door. We couldn't go in. Mom kept cooking in the kitchen ... it was all a mystery. We peeked in every time she opened the door to come in and out but could see very little.

We always had to do chores, morning and night, no matter if there were lots of guys around or not or if it was Christmas Eve. The girls milked the cows and separated the milk. We still were not allowed to peak in the living room yet.

Christmas Eve finally arrived and secretly Evelyn and Mom must have placed our gifts under the tree too. When supper was finally over and chores all done, the door was opened - wow! So beautiful! - we finally got to look in to the living room. Evelyn had the room beautifully clean and shining, and streamers up, and the tree decorated. When we finally got in the living room we all gathered around and only the lucky ones got the chairs and couch, but I usually got the floor. Daddy read the Christmas story. What a beautiful story but it was lost on me, cause all I could see was the gifts.

Then gifts were given out - all at once - rip rip rip and tear - in a couple minutes they were all opened, and we hugged the couple things we got, which was usually 2 things - socks or some clothing, and a small gift. I was always disappointed cause it seemed so small, but it was a big thing for Mom. Money was very short. Then the candy was brought out and the nuts, and the mess got even more messy, but it was a happy time. All gathered around the pot belly heater.

We never had fancy things to decorate with. Once we got a few round shiny balls to hang on the Christmas tree, but they broke so easily. I don't remember ever having electric lights because we never had electricity on the farm.

We never had a tree stand either. It was always a problem how to hold it up. Sometimes they nailed it on a board, sometimes put it in a bucket filled with rocks, but always it seemed to want to tip over. Tinsel was the best part. We hung tinsel on all the branches and on some of the streamers. We thought it was beautiful. Once we made popcorn and threaded it on thread - didn't stay on very well. Sometimes we also made paper chains, but never had coloured paper to make them from.

One year, we girls all got embroidery to do. I was thrilled. They said I was too small to do it, but I thought I did a pretty good job. Guess I was out to prove a point and was very careful. Later it seems most of us girls took a turn at wanting to make the living room look nice each year.

The Basement Goes Under the House

Our house was very small, and it didn't have a very big basement. The basement was just dug out hole and had dirt walls and was very dark and damp. It was very scary to go down to get vegetables, or coal for the stove. Yes coal! We used wood and coal stoves for heat and for the cook stove. It was a very dirty job to go down stairs and break the coal into small enough pieces so that we could carry it up in buckets for Mom to keep the stove burning.

One day Mom said to Daddy "It sure would be nice to have a basement with cement walls." She drew up a plan and showed him what it would look like. One corner would be a cement room for water (a cistern). We could melt wax and paint the walls, so they would hold water and the rain would fill it with water from the eave's troughs. Then she could use a hand pump in the kitchen and have water to wash without having to have it hauled up from the creek. When there wasn't enough rain to fill the cistern, and the water got low, Daddy could pump a tank full of water from the creek to fill it. It would be nice not to have to haul all the water we needed to clean, cook and do laundry.

The basement would have a separate room for coal. Daddy could bring a load of coal to the window in the room, and using a wooden chute, he would fill the room with coal for the winter. He could get enough to last all winter and would not have to go get more when it was very cold out. There were to be shelves to store all the fruit and vegetables that Mom and we girls canned.

The cement stairway from the outside would be used for storing hams. There was a 3' X 3' landing at the door, which was meant to be an exit and way of getting in from the outside of the house, but Mom found it was a cool place to hang hams when they were curing. Daddy would smoke them by rubbing smoke salt on and then hanging them to cure. This stairway had a door into the foundation of the house and a door at the top of the stairs, so was closed off from outside so cats and creatures couldn't get in to eat the hams. It was also cool, and the meat would keep a long time.

Well, Daddy agreed that it was a good idea to put a basement under the house. It was an exciting day when he started. He had three hired men, who were French (only one could speak English), who started to dig. They dug out a few places, so they could put a jack under and put some big logs under to hold the house up when they dug out the dirt and sand. They were half way done when the men started to laugh and talk in French. Daddy said, "What are you laughing at?" The man who could speak English said, "They had just got out of jail for robbing and hurting an old lady. They thought it would be funny if they found a bunch of money in the basement." Daddy looked at Mom in shock. They just remembered they had hidden money there a long time ago. Daddy called to Mom to come to the bedroom. "Do you remember where it was hidden?" "Yes," Mom said, "but we don't dare let them know we have any money, or they will rob us too." So, Daddy told Mom to make a pot of coffee. He took the men up to the kitchen and kept the men talking and drinking coffee until Mom had time to crawl down into the basement and climb up and get the can of money off of the beam and hide it in the bedroom. When they were talking about finding money they had been standing right under the beam that Mom had put the jar of money on.

The men dug a big hole behind the house and then started to dig out under the house. They used our pair of mules, named Jack and Jenny, with a handheld scoop. They tipped the scoop up and held it tight and made the mules start to pull it. The scoop would fill up like when we dig for our houses today – only with a mechanical digger. The mules would pull the full scoop out of the hole and the men would tip the scoop up and dump the sand and go back for more. It was a long hard job, but finally it was completed. Then, Daddy put up the forms and they were ready for cement. The men set up the cement mixer and started to mix cement and using a wheelbarrow they started to fill the forms. We girls took the mules and wagon and gathered small rocks. Daddy then dropped in some small rocks and that helped save on cement costs and made it stronger. When the basement was all poured we waited a few days before Daddy had the men pour the floor. It was an exciting day when we all got to go down there and walk on the new cement floor.

Now that the basement was done we had to treat the cistern walls with wax. Daddy bought many, many boxes of wax at the town store. Mom melted them, and the men put a ladder down from the trap door which daddy cut in the kitchen floor. The men went down with the melted wax and a brush. All day mom melted wax, and the men brushed it on. When it finally had many coats of wax, they decided it was time to try it out. The eve troughs were designed so that the rain water would run in to the cistern. How exciting it was to hear the first water run in. Daddy had installed a hand pump by the sink and we truly had "running water" for the first time.

"But we still had to carry out the dirty water," Mom lamented. So, Daddy put a pipe from the kitchen sink out the side of the house. This was OK in the summer, but in the winter, we still had to carry water out.

After mom did a lot of complaining, the next summer daddy dug a septic system. He dug a big hole down the hill from the house and lined it with stone so that it wouldn't cave in. A pipe was put under ground from the house sink into it. Then they put poles and burlap on top and covered it with sand. Now we were living in the lap of luxury.

All we had to do was to pump and we had water and then pour the dirty water in the sink and it ran away, no dirty water to carry out. It couldn't get much better than that! Now, all the water we had to carry was what we drank and cooked with. It was wonderful!

A couple of years after the septic system was in, the top began to cave in. The poles had rotted. We were to stay away for fear of falling in. One day our three-month old puppy was missing, it's mother Shep was frantic. We listened and heard it crying. After a bit of searching we discovered the sounds were coming from the septic pit. "But how can we get it?" we all yelled. The men took pity on us and the puppy, and with the tractor, made a hole big enough for Walter to go in head first down the "smelly" hole with a rope tied around his waist and rescued the puppy. We bathed the puppy many times to get all of the smell off of him.

Daddy was never very good at cleaning up his mess, so the sand was not backfilled around our new cement basement for a long time. It was great to dig and play in. Mom warned us to never to go into the hole beside the cement walls. "It may cave in on you," she would say. Well, we were not very good at listening. One day we were having so much fun digging that we went way in beside the cement where Mom had said not to go. All of a sudden, the sand started to fall. It fell on top of my brother Earl. It half covered him. Hazel and I screamed and started to dig with our hands. The faster we dug the more the sand fell. Soon the men came running. We were thankful they were close by. They were big and strong and soon dug Earl out. That was a very close call. If they hadn't gotten him out when they did, he would have died. We really were in a lot of trouble with Mom for that, but we learned our lesson. We must obey Mom, even if we think it would be fun to do what she said not to do. It never pays to disobey. We almost lost our brother because we disobeyed. Daddy right away got the mules and a scoop and backfilled the basement so that couldn't happen again, but they stopped before the hole behind the house was filled. We still had lots of sand to play in.

One morning we saw our dog, Shep, digging into the bank. She dug a very deep cave. The next morning, we saw her coming out of it. Earl and I ran out to look. Deep in the cave were a bunch of little puppies. We tried to reach in to get them, but our arms were too short. She was very smart. She dug it deep enough, so we couldn't reach them. They came out when they were big enough to play with.

Bed Bugs

Bed bugs were a real problem. I don't know how we got them. Some think that birds nesting in the eve of houses carried the bugs with them from house to house. The bugs hid in the little cracks in the mattress and came out at night and fed on you while you sleep. In the morning, we would wake up with many bite bumps.

One night, Daddy had taken a couple of us girls to church. When we got home we found some mattresses in the yard. Ruth and Evelyn had just gotten tired of the bugs and decided they would get rid of them. They hauled all the mattresses into the yard and soaked them with gasoline and kerosene. "This," they said," would for sure kill all the bugs." The bedding was washed in very hot water. I was sent to sweep out a granary. We piled some straw on the granary floor in the corners, and with freshly washed blankets, we made our beds for the summer. The mattresses stayed outside, in the sun, most of the summer and by summer's end the smell of gas had gone. We scoured the attic, by pouring kerosene into the cracks in the wood floor, to kill any bugs that might be there. Then we painted. Finally, we moved back in before the fall chill came. The only complaint Daddy had was that all the kerosene could make the house go up in smoke. We were thankful the treatments we used did the trick and got rid of the bugs - or so we thought!

Birthday Party

Mom and Dad never made a fuss over birthdays. In fact, I'm sure I never got a birthday gift from them. We girls usually tried to make a cake when someone had a birthday, but we didn't usually have a party. When Daddy turned 50 we made a cake and put "Happy Half Century" on it. He was so upset that he didn't want to eat any. We didn't want to be mean, we were just teasing. He really dreaded getting old and didn't want a reminder.

A Birthday Wish

Birthdays are persistent
They're sure to come each year
It will dare to come again soon
You never need to fear!

They make us feel much older
Tho' this is surely true,
It marks another milestone
The Lord has seen us through.

But we can feel so thankful
For His own watchful care.
And trust if He should tarry
We'll feel Him always there.

And now we want to wish you
On this your special day,
The best that we could wish you
For health and happiness, we pray.

May you each day feel courage
For what ahead you lies
until the Lord shall call us
And we would upward FLY

Evelyn and I were the only ones who had a birthday in the summer. Since she was away from home by the time the rest of us were big enough to plan anything, I was the one who usually got the party. Summer was boring at times and we struggled to find something fun to do. One year, when August 8 came, no one said a word about my birthday. In fact, they ignored me and sent me to do all the chores they could that took me away from the house – to the well, to the ice house, to the barn, to feed the chickens etc. Well, I would not remind them that it was my birthday! I cried and cried! "They don't love me enough to wish me Happy Birthday!", I thought. Well, I was sent to go to the well again. When I came back everyone yelled, "Surprise". The neighbour girls had come over and I found out the reason I was sent to do so many chores. It was so that my sisters could plan my party. They hadn't forgotten at all, they just wanted to surprise me. That was so nice of them.

Harvest

By the first part of July, Daddy was eyeing the hay fields. It took a lot of food to feed all his cows and sheep over the winter. We had a few hay fields to cut. The men usually cut the hay with the mower and after it was dry, one of us would take the mules, and the rake, to rake it into windrows. Then the men would come alongside

the windrow and fork the hay into the big hayrack. Then they would drive to the stack yard where they forked it into a huge haystack. When the oat fields were ready to harvest they would be cut and made into oat sheaves. Later the big kids [and even Mom] would stand 6 – 7 sheaves on end in a pile called a stook. This let them finish drying and protected them in case of rain. Later most of these oat sheaves were hauled to the stack yard too. This was done with the wheat too. When the wheat sheaves were all done and dry, Daddy would start the trashing machine and gather the grain into bins. The straw was blown into a huge straw stack, to be used later for animal bedding. We loved to play in the straw stacks but had to wait a few weeks for the straw to settle down and pack, otherwise we could sink into it and smother.

We had a thrashing machine but many of the farmers did not have one. Neighbours helped each other and went from farm to farm doing threshing. We little

kids had to go out to the fields at mid-morning and mid-afternoon with lunch and drinks for the men. Oh, how I hated that job! The thistles and stubble hurt our little bare feet and grasshoppers flew up and hit our bare legs. It hurt a lot. There was a great deal of work to prepare dinner and supper as well. Often during harvest, we fed a dozen men. The harvest work was so hard, and the men were very hungry and ate a great deal. We always tried to have lots of meat, potatoes and a dessert [usually pie or apple crisp]. When corn was ready we cooked huge canners of corn on the cob and served this as well as peas, beans, and cucumbers. Of course, there were always pickles [usually dill or beet]. When supper was over, and the men relaxed, we began on the dishes. Dishes were all done by hand in pans of hot water we had put on the old cook stove. Our days were pretty full, with chores, but we always found time to play. We spent many an hour wading in the creek or making rafts to float around pretending to be Huckleberry Finn. We watched muskrats swimming around and enjoyed hearing them slap their tail in warning when they discovered us nearby. The creek didn't flow much except when we had a big rain, so the weeds grew thick. There were also tiny water flowers that poked their heads above water. Blue dragonflies were also in abundance floating around above the water. Many frogs hopped about and croaked. It was a delightful place to play. The sun was very hot, and Mom would say – "My, my, I am so worried about you having a sunstroke in the heat. Put on a hat." We would reluctantly obey, then ditch them as soon as we were out of her sight. They were such a bother! I still get goose bumps when I think of the many coloured snakes we saw slithering across the water and disappearing in the reeds on the banks. We knew where to find the bird nests in the grass, but we stayed away from them, so we didn't endanger the babies.

Sometimes we got our pillow sack floats and went to the neighbours' pasture to enjoy a swim. After a swim we always looked each other over to pick off any bloodsuckers that attached themselves to us.

Sometimes we hung around the barn and played in the sun with the baby kittens or climbed like monkeys all over the barn.

(*Shirley*)

On days we felt adventurous we climbed on to old Nelly and Jenny and roamed for miles through the pastures. But, always, we managed to be home in time to do chores like feeding the chickens, milking the cows and help make supper.

The Sheep

Every spring as the days got warmer, the sheep had to have their heavy wool coats sheared off. Usually Daddy hired men to come to do it. They pitched a tent in the trees. This area was off bounds for us. Mom didn't trust them. It was bad enough to have them around us for meals. For shearing, Daddy hung a huge burlap bag from the rafters in the barn. As each sheep was sheared, the wool fleece was tossed into the bag. When it was half full, someone had to climb in to the bag to pack the wool tight by stomping it down. Once you got in the bag you couldn't get out until it was full. You had to duck as each fleece came in, then tramp it down and wait for the next dirty fleece to come. The boys usually did this. I did it once. After that I made myself scarce until someone was already in the bag and only then came to watch the shearing. These bags were about 4 feet across and 12 feet long. They made a great place to play before Daddy got around to shipping them to the blanket factory.

The sheep always got sheep ticks. A bit later in the summer, Daddy got a big trough and filled it with water and some stuff to kill ticks. The sheep would be herded down a chute and up a ramp. Then they were pushed off the ramp and into the medicated water. Once they were very wet, they were fished out and let go. This took care of the tick problem.

Chickens Arrive

Every spring Mom started thinking about what kind of chicks to get and how many she wanted to raise. The brooder house had to be white washed to disinfect it and it had to be cleaned and fresh sand put down. Then we put a layer of fresh dry straw. Then Mom ordered her chicks and a few baby turkeys. She was told what day to expect them to come in on the train. Daddy would meet the train and hurry home with the chicks. They came from Moose Jaw and were only a couple of days old. We loved the little yellow balls of fluff. Mom had the oil brooder stove going for a couple of days to get the brooder house well warmed for the chicks. We loved to go with Mom and put them in their new home. We picked up each chick, dipped its beak in the water dish, and then sat it under the brooder hood. Soon they were all running around or nestled in the fresh straw we had put down for them. At first, we spent a lot of hours playing with them, or watching them learn to eat out of the tiny little feeders. They grew fast and by the end of summer they were big, beautiful white chickens.

While it was always best to buy baby chicks it was fun too, to hatch some as well. Since Mom always kept a couple of roosters, most of the eggs we got were fertile. So, as soon as we found a clucking chicken we would tell Mom. When a chicken decided she wanted to sit on eggs she would begin to walk around with her feathers all fluffed out and make a clucking sound. Often, we would find her as we gathered eggs. She just wouldn't jump off the nest and made a fuss when we tried to gather the eggs from under her. So, Mom would set up a box for her to have as a nest. After 21 days the eggs would hatch. By day 19 and 20 we would slip out an egg from under her and hold it to our ear. We were listening for that little tap, tap, tap they made as they pecked their way out of the egg.

After all the little balls of fluff were hatched, Mom moved them to a little house with a chicken wire pen around it. There was an opening along one side just big enough for them to go in and get out of the rain if they needed to.

We had fun feeding them with cottage cheese, hardboiled eggs and ground grain. It was also fun to see the mamma chicken feeding her babies by picking up bits and dropping them on the ground in front of them. Then she would peck away at the ground to show them how to pick up the food. The chicks grew quickly. It wasn't long before they could fend for themselves. We then opened the pen and let them have free range in the yard with all the other chickens.

Saturdays, Mom would say, "Go and catch a couple of chickens for tomorrow." Chicken is what we often had for Sunday lunch. It was hard to catch them since they ran loose in the yard. We got a big bucket of grain and the chickens would all come running. We took a long piece of wire [about 4 feet long] and bent the end into a hook. This we could quietly slip under the chicken that we wanted to catch, place the hook around a leg and pull. Then we could grab it. We then would go to Mom to okay our choice. Once she agreed with our choice, she would send us out to the woodpile to chop their heads off. Once we chopped their heads off, we tossed them on the ground to flop around and bleed out before we took them to clean. One time we went back a few minutes later and no chicken was to be seen. We looked and looked! Finally, we found it, stomping in circles, his head hanging from a tiny piece of skin. He was dead, so I don't know what happened, but it was a freaky thing to happen.

A lot of the chickens were killed in the fall. Daddy sold them in town to people who couldn't have their own. We kept some since we needed the meat, and some were kept for the eggs they laid.

One winter we often found a few chickens dead when we went to feed them. What happened to these healthy-looking chickens? One day we found out. While we were at school, and the men were in town, Mom was home alone and decided to go look after her chickens. She got a lot of pleasure from taking care of the chickens. She opened the door and got a shock. There in plain daylight was Mr. Weasel in his beautiful white fur coat. She closed the door quietly and tried to think what she could do. Now she understood what had happened to so many of her beautiful hens. She blocked the opening in the wall (the chickens went out through this opening to reach their pen to sit in the sunshine) and went to the house. She got the .22, found a bullet and marched right back to her hen house. Now, she had never ever shot a gun before. She was actually afraid of guns, and normally, she wouldn't hurt a thing. But, Mr. Weasel was different. He was killing her beloved chickens. So, she opened the door quietly, put the barrel of the gun in, aimed and pulled the trigger and "BANG" Mr. Weasel lay dead on the ground. Then Mom fed the chickens and talked quietly to them, so they would settle down. She then picked up Mr. Weasel by the tail and went back to the house. When we all came home Mom picked up Mr. Weasel by the tail and said, "Well, he won't get any more of my chickens this old weasel!" We all cheered at our brave little Mom for daring to shoot the gun even when she was afraid.

Sickness Hits

We all had the usual childhood diseases. When we had chicken pox, Mom put a dish of soda paste on the kitchen table and when the itch got too bad we plastered our spots with soda paste. It didn't help much, but we were willing to try anything that might help at all.

I well remember when I got mumps. I was hoping that it was going to miss me when everyone else was getting sick, but one morning I got up and came downstairs. I wasn't feeling well, but I thought if I pretended to be well I wouldn't get the mumps. Mom took one look at me and laughed so hard she cried and had to sit down. I was so insulted! I still didn't know why she was laughing. Finally, she said, "Your face is as round as an apple. You look so funny." I looked in the mirror and sure enough I had the mumps. I was tucked in to Mom's bed which was by the living room and was nice and warm. There I stayed for a couple of days until the swelling started to go down. Bed did feel very good, and I didn't have to pretend anymore.

One year we got the itch. Our backs were so itchy we used to form a circle with chairs and sit in a circle and scratch each other's backs. It lasted most of the winter until Daddy talked to the doctor. The doctor gave Daddy some lotion that stung like fire and some stinky cream for the less hardy ones. Hazel was determined to use the lotion. She rubbed it on for ages and it burned so bad. She would dance around hoping it would help it not to burn so bad. Anyway, I'm not sure if the treatment helped or if the itch just went away.

Daddy read a lot of Reader's Digest magazines. Often, they had articles about food. One time he read that white flour was bad for you and that you should really use whole-wheat flour. So, he refused to buy white flour. He said white flour was poison. He cleaned up the mill he used for making chop for the animals and ground up wheat. That was our flour. Mom was pretty upset, but she tolerated his decision for a while. It made awful bread and even worse pancakes and cakes. We just couldn't eat them. Weeks later, when her flour supply was low, Mom put her foot down and said she wanted white flour. For a while, to pacify Daddy, she added a bit of cracked wheat to the bread. It tasted okay. Finally, the rest of the homemade flour was fed to the baby chicks. They thought it was great. And we were only too glad to feed it to them. They were welcome to it.

Then Daddy read that blackstrap molasses was a very good tonic. He went to town and home he came with a big jar of – you guessed it – blackstrap molasses.

I obeyed once and took a spoonful. There was no way he was going to get any more in me! Some of the others were a bit braver but not much of the molasses got taken. Mom ended up adding a bit to each batch of bread. That was tolerable.

————

One spring jaundice was going around. One by one we got sick. Our skin and eyes turned yellow. I was so sure I would not get it. So, even though I was sick I did my chores and went to school. One day, at school, someone looked at my eyes and said – "your eyes are yellow." I denied it and pretended to feel quite well. But when I got home Mom took one look at me and got after me for not telling her. Again, I was put to bed. It sure felt good because I really was sick.

————

Mom suffered from gallstones and had a number of attacks. But, like me, she didn't say much so we often didn't know when she was sick. One summer day, she had an attack. She tried to keep working, but it was so bad she had to sit down. Evelyn and Daddy took one look at her and got her into bed. By this time, she was groaning with pain. Evelyn did what she could while Daddy rushed for the doctor. Earl and I were terrified. We went to the barn to play but we couldn't play – we were sure our Mother was dying. Hours later, she finally felt relief. I think the doctor told her what he thought it was, and what foods to avoid, because she never had a real bad spell again. Years later she did have her gallbladder removed.

———

A little while later Daddy was on Nelly, our grey horse. Mr. Cooper drove into the yard, so Daddy rode up to talk to him. They had talked for a while when Mr. Cooper accidentally bumped the car horn. Nelly spooked and jumped straight sideways. Daddy landed on the ground. He spent weeks flat on his back. His back never was good after that. He had a lot of pain. It was a nasty fall. Once again, we were terrified. We thought for sure he was dying.

———

One summer Hazel spent a couple of weeks at Uncle Bill's farm. She had a wonderful time, but when she came home she got sick. She was determined to hold up her end of the chores. She helped milk cows and had started to turn the milk separator when Mom realized how sick she really was. I was told to stop working on supper and finish the milk separating. Mom took Hazel to the living room couch and made her lay down. She finally gave in. Hazel lay there for weeks. The doctor was called quite a few times. We were so worried she would die. Finally, Evelyn cornered the doctor – "What are we dealing with here?" she demanded. "I don't really know." he told her. "Yes, you do, even if you don't have tests back. You aren't leaving here until you tell me." Finally, he said, "I think it is typhoid fever." The test results came back, and it was confirmed to be typhoid fever. They took her to Assiniboia hospital, where she was for weeks. We all were quarantined and had to get weekly shots from the doctor. Evelyn wanted to disinfect everything in sight. She boiled bedding, totally cleaned the living room, then painted and papered the walls. Thankfully, no one else got typhoid. We came to the conclusion that it had come from contaminated well water at Uncle Bill's farm. After weeks in the hospital, Hazel finally came home. She was very skinny, and all her hair fell out from the high fever, but she lived!

I was in grade 9 when Hazel took sick again. She had a strange rash and the doctor put her in the hospital. One day at school the telephone rang - they had just put in a party line telephone. Uncle Dewey answered, and it was for me. I was terrified, I'd never even listened on the telephone, let alone talk on one. A party line is when the whole neighborhood was on the same line. Each had a ring code, like one long and one short, or 2 longs and 2 short, but when we heard a call come through we could all pick up the receiver and listen. Try as I would, I could not make out anything other than that it was Evelyn on the phone. She was calling to see how Hazel was, but I was so scared by the telephone that I couldn't even understand her. Uncle Dewey finally took the phone and got the message.

Sometimes we put the mules out to pasture in the small pasture close to the house. Here they were easy to catch but could still get to eat some of the tender green grass they loved. One day Bud took them out to the pasture. He took off their halters. Then he hit Jenny lightly to get her to run away so he could shut the gate and not worry about them getting out. Jenny didn't think that was a great idea and kicked up her heels. She hit Bud in the side of his head. When he finally came to, he walked to the house with blood running down his face. He was rushed to the doctor who said that if it had been a quarter of an inch closer to his temple he would have been killed. We were so thankful to the Lord for sparing his life.

Getting more new Siblings

One day in May Daddy said, "Come on I want you to get your nightgowns. You are going to spend the night at Scotts." He had a rebellion on his hands. Her house was very small and crowded. We liked her daughter, Jean, who was my age and her Mom, Vera, was very nice. However, we were afraid of her dad and the thought of sleeping at their house was not appealing at all. When Daddy had his mind made up we did what we were told. So, we piled into the truck and went the half mile north to Scotts. We had no idea why we had to go. Then just as we were getting ready for bed the truck drove in. It was Daddy. "I've changed my mind," he said. "Come home." We were overjoyed and wasted no time getting our things. When we got home, Daddy marched us into the bedroom. There was Mom, in bed with a tiny baby boy. What a surprise! A woman named Mrs. Osborn had assisted Dr. Welsh in the delivery. "What is his name?" we asked. "We haven't decided yet" Mom said. So, for a week the two hired men, George and Herb, would come in and say, "Hi George", "Hi Herb". By the end of the week it was established his name would be George Herbert. George was a delight. We welcomed our little brother with open arms. He was very young when he started to sing. And over the years he used his wonderful singing voice to honour the Lord. *(I was 6 years old when George was born)*

A couple of years later Daddy took Mom to town right after Christmas to stay at Mrs. Day's Nursing Home. "She is tired and needs rest." we were told. A couple of days later Hazel and I went in for a quick visit. We could not understand why she couldn't rest at home. We were in the store waiting for Daddy to pick us up. One of Mom's friends, Mrs. Wangan, said, "Is your Mom going to have her baby?" We were so indignant! This busybody saying things about our Mother! "No," we said, "she's just having a rest." I never forgave her for that. Well, New Year's Eve Daddy went to town. We were in bed by the time he got home. When we woke up he said, "Well you have a new baby sister." "She has long black hair." It took a lot of convincing, but eventually we believed him. He wasn't just teasing. It was really true. I can't begin to say how much pleasure our little sister, Linda, gave us. She was always the favourite among us all and still is. *(I was 9 years old when Linda was born)*

Blacksmith

Daddy was a very good blacksmith. I was always fascinated to see how he could heat things up in the forge then shape them the way he needed to, by putting them on the anvil and hitting it with a hammer. He would build a fire in the forge with special coal then would have one of us stand there and slowly turn the handle of the fan that blew air under the coals to keep them burning very hot. It was a job I sure didn't like. If I was around to watch, I often got given the job. It wasn't hard, but I had to stand still to do it. That I found hard. He fixed parts for machinery, but he also did his own horse shoeing. He would trim their hoofs, then carefully nail on the shoes once they were shaped to the right shape for each horse. It never ceased to amaze me how they could put nails into the horse's feet and the horse just stood still. Daddy loved his horses and took very good care of them.

The forge was also used to heat up the branding irons when they branded cattle. Branding was a big job. Every summer all the new calves had to be marked with a brand. All the cattle were rounded up and put in the corral. Then they carefully let out the older ones and kept only the ones they needed to brand.

Old Nelly always had a rider on her to help direct the animals and catch any that got away. It had to be someone who was good at roping. The lasso was tossed, animal caught, then one of the men would grab it and throw it down to the ground and tie its legs together. While this was happening, another man ran over with a hot branding iron and branded the hip of the calf. If it was a male – then he was doctored, given an antibiotic shot. He then was let go out with the older cattle.

Branding was hard work. It took most of the day. All available men worked. Sometimes some neighbours came to help as well. We girls had to help make food. After all that hard work, the men sure ate a lot. It was our job to be sure there was enough food and lots of coffee for the men.

Quilt making

We got a lot of used clothes given to us by our city cousins. Much of it was of no use for us to wear. A few things we were able to use when Evelyn picked the garments apart, and after pressing the pieces, she was able to make a coat or something out of it. The rest got sorted out into wool and garbage. The wool garments were all taken apart to remove all interfacing, then packaged up to send to the Moose Jaw woollen mills to be made into blankets.

Evelyn and Mom also used to make patchwork quilts. Once the tops were all sewn together, they used to set up the quilting frame in the living room. Each corner was propped up on a chair back. It filled the room almost wall to wall. Then came the tiresome job of quilting. Sometimes they invited some neighbour ladies over for a quilting bee. That was nice because they could finish a quilt in a day. They did a lot of visiting as they stitched away, and of course, there was always coffee and cake. While the women quilted we kids often played on the floor under the quilt frame. All we saw was the backside of the quilt, so it was a pleasant surprise to see the top when it was finished. Just like it will be when we get to heaven. We will see the bright side and all the Lord was accomplishing when we were going through trials while here on earth. We will see it was all for a reason.

(photo- wool carder)

The padding in the quilt was always wool. Mom used to send us out in the summer with a bag to walk the fence line to pick the bits of wool off the barbed wire fence - left there when the sheep rubbed against it. We also had to pull the wool off all the sheep that died, before the men took the carcass out to the bone pile at the end of the pasture. Oh! how I hated that job! Some years we lost so many sheep to coyotes that we had a lot of wool to pick. Mom would wash this wood carefully then spread it out in the sun on a frame covered by window screen. The air would dry the wool quickly. Once the wool was dry, we then spent hours feeding it in to the wool carder where we made it into wool bats for quilts.

One winter Evelyn saw an ad in the paper for quilt patches -- $20 – you were to get 2,500 quilt patches and a 20-piece cutlery set. They figured how many quilts they could make out of 2,500 quilt patches and we sure could use cutlery. The order was sent in. Two weeks later a parcel arrived. Evelyn had decided on some quilt designs and was ready to set to work. The parcel was surprisingly small. They tore it open excitedly. There on the table lay a pile of tiny, tiny pieces of material. The largest was about an inch square. The cutlery was tiny spoons pressed out of tin and totally useless as well. It was a lesson learned. The whole package went in to the garbage, and for weeks there was a lot of grumbling about dishonest people.

Earl

Earl was always a very special brother. We had a lot of good times together. He was always trying to be grown up beyond his years. One day he spent a long time looking in the mirror. He was looking for signs of manhood. All of a sudden, he came running excitedly to Mom. "Mom I found a hair on my chest." he yelled. Ruth told him she could tell him how to make hair grow on his chest. "For two days you rub salt on your chest. Then the third day you pass a glass of water by and when the hair sticks out to get a drink, you grab it split it and tie it in a knot." Earl wasn't impressed.

One winter he had his heart set on getting a pet. First it was a bunny. "How can I catch a bunny Dad?" He asked "Well you sprinkle pepper on a rock. And when the bunny comes along he will smell it. The pepper will make it sneeze. When it sneezes, it will knock itself out. Then you run and grab it before it comes to," Daddy told him. For days he busied himself by putting pepper on rocks. When he got tired of looking for bunnies he decided he would settle for a bird. They were plentiful. Daddy told him, "Take a dry crust. Tie a string to it. Then lay it on the ground and stand back. When the bird swallows the crust, pull the string and you just caught a bird." Well, needless to say, he never caught a bird either. When he was in high school he was a cowboy. One of his teachers came to the farm and made a movie of branding cattle.

———

For a while Earl was into bikes. Somehow, he got an old bike and was always taking it apart and putting it back together. One time he had a tire that wouldn't keep air in. He decided to pump it up to find out where it leaked. He pumped and pumped. He didn't realize he was putting too much air into it until all of a sudden it went bang and blew up. What a noise! The funny part was that it went bang just as the man in Daddy's story pulled the trigger and murdered someone. I thought Daddy was going to go into orbit! It took a while before we noticed Earl with his long face looking at his tire with the side blown out. We all felt kind of bad for Earl that he had ruined his tire.

———

Mom and Dad Go to Trail, B.C.

When I was about 13, Dad and Mom decided to go to Trail, B.C., to see Dad's folks. Grandma and Grandpa McPeek were getting old. They felt that time was getting on and we didn't know how long we would have them. I was the oldest girl at home at the time, so I had to cook and clean for the men and hired hands. I did the milking, cooking and cleaning as well as the laundry and caring for the chickens. I did very well, until I decided to make a lemon pie. I did like Mom always did for pumpkin pies. I partially baked the shell, put in the filling and put meringue on top. Then I browned the meringue. It looked delicious, but when the men handed the partially cooked crust back for a refill – I was mortified. I didn't realize that the crust wouldn't finish baking when I browned the meringue. I got teased for months about making refillable pie shells, but at 13, I did pretty well taking over the household chores.

Art Comes a Calling

My oldest sister, Evelyn, was always very special. She was the best sister any girl could want. Whatever we needed, she would do for us. She curled our hair, sewed dresses for us and she even made me a coat that I wore until I couldn't squeeze into it any more. So, it was really something when the boys started to call on her. One day Art came. I don't know where she met him, but we didn't like him much. He might become more important to her than we were. He came more and more often, and he just didn't know when to go home. Sometimes we would complain to Mom. "We want to go to bed, Mom, and Art won't go home." Mom said, "just take him his hat." Well, he would turn his hat around in his hand and tell Evelyn what a nice hat he had, but still didn't leave.

One night everyone wanted to go to bed so we banished them to the kitchen while we went to bed. After they thought we were all asleep they tiptoed in to the living room to look at the calendar and then went back to the kitchen. Bud, my big brother, jumped up to see if they made any mark on the calendar. He was the smart one. He knew they would likely be getting married and wondered if they marked the date on the calendar. No mark appeared so he was none the wiser. Then one cold day Art came to spend the night. The next morning everyone was a flutter. What was the matter? Hazel whispered, "Look at Evelyn's hand." It was wash day and Mom had the big copper boiler on the stove to heat wash water. The boiler had sprung a leak and Evelyn was rubbing a bar of homemade soap on it to plug the hole. I shyly slipped in by the wood box, so I could get a glimpse of her hand. Wow. The most beautiful ring I had ever seen was on my sister's finger. I didn't really know what it was all about, but I was sure excited.

As the days went by, I found out she would be leaving us. I was pretty sad. How could he take her away? She was my sister. A couple months before the wedding, Mom, Evelyn and Daddy went to Moose Jaw. Mom didn't ever go, and I didn't know why she was going now. There was some mystery in the air. Evelyn came home with a pile of bags. Some brand-new dresses and a wedding dress which we discovered later because she never showed it to us at the time. I can still see her sitting on the edge of the table swinging her foot so relaxed as if she went to the city every day to buy clothes. It was all too wonderful for me to take in.

The day eventually came. She spent the last few days at her future in-laws' home to help with the preparations. I had a brand-new dress to wear, but I didn't want to wear because it wasn't comfortable. It was a bit tight and besides why should I dress up to see her go away? The weather was very rainy. We had trouble getting away on time and traveling was very slow because of the mud. We arrived at the wedding just as they were pronounced man & wife. I guess I was spared at least some of the agony of seeing her snatched away. She looked so beautiful! Everyone came out of the church and shook their hands and then we all went over to Art's father's place where the big hip-roof barn had been converted into a banquet hall.

Oh, it was so big. I had never seen a nicer place. I thought, "This would make a nice house." They had streamers of crape paper up to the rafters and tables were dressed beautifully in white tablecloths.

After a delicious meal, (Grandma Manske was such a good cook) and speeches were over they were walking around talking and getting ready to say farewell when someone came in with a wheel barrow. They put Evelyn in this and they gave her a ride. I wanted to run and help her. How could they put my sister with her pretty dress in there? Well, when the ride was over, and she and Art made a mad dash for their car. Some of us had fixed up the car real fancy. The big boys had tied some tin cans and old shoes on to it and tucked them under, so they could not be seen before it was driven away. Hazel and I tied a roll of toilet paper on. We had visions of it unrolling for miles behind as they traveled. Well, Art went off spinning his wheels. Mud flew everywhere. Tin cans and old shoes bounced away, but our roll of toilct paper lay limply on the ground. The rain had wet the paper and it never even unrolled. We were disappointed and home we went. I had a big empty place in my heart cause my sister was gone now.

Carolann Arrives after a sleigh ride

As time went on, Evelyn and Art became the proud parents of a sweet baby girl, Carolann. Winter was long and with lots of snow. Most roads were blocked with snow banks. Time came for Evelyn to have her baby. Roads to Coronach were blocked so Art took her to Scobey, Montana by sleigh, where Carolann was born.

Another day, a few years later, Daddy had gone to town and wasn't home when Art came to tell us that baby Arnold had arrived. Mom was really excited. Before long Daddy came driving down the road. Quickly we put Mom into a chair dusted her hair with flour to make it grey, put some knitting in her hands and set her in a chair. When Daddy walked in he was startled. "What is the matter?" Daddy asked. "I feel old. I'm Grandma again", Mom said with a quivering voice. Daddy got mad. "We aren't old." We all thought it was funny, but Daddy didn't laugh. He had a lot of trouble admitting he was getting old.

The Minister Calls

One hot summer day at home everyone was feeling tired and had a rest. I couldn't rest, so having an unusual spurt of energy, and I decided to churn butter. The house was a mess, but that didn't bother us. It was too hot to work, and Mom had the flu. I was almost finished the butter when I looked out the window. "Hey girls, the minister, Mr. and Mrs. Weise are coming." Now everyone looked around the house and it really was such a mess. Everyone joined in to clean, but it was too late. They had arrived before we got much accomplished. The girls sheepishly led them in to the bedroom where mom was in bed. Poor mom, she was so embarrassed at the state of the house. All she could think of was the mess and the smell that came up from the basement. The potatoes were rotting because they had weathered the long winter, and it now was spring, so that needed cleaning out. The big girls tried to get me to forget the butter and help them clean while they were in the bedroom. But I self-righteously said, "NO, I'm making butter." I felt good that they found me working. Soon the minister came out and left his wife visiting and he helped clean. I can imagine our ears should have burned when they went home. I could just hear them say, "Those lazy girls and their mom sick too." Well, as soon as they left, Mom jumped up and we began to clean in earnest, from potatoes in the basement to the attic bedrooms. We worked hard and with determination, but did we have a clean house after!

The Shoe Salesman

Mom was always polite, even if a salesman came. She didn't usually buy, but she couldn't bring herself to tell him to leave. Mr. Henderson was selling Watkins products, which mom sometimes bought, but this time he came and said he had a new line. Waterproof shoes. They were nice shiny shoes and I could just see how proud I would be of our Daddy if he could buy a pair, but we didn't have the money. Well, he talked and talked, and was just leaving the house when his car started to roll down the hill. He had forgotten to put the brake on. He ran to try to catch it but couldn't catch up. It rolled down the hill and into the creek. I can still see it there, with water up to the windows and open boxes of those shoes, nice shiny brown shoes floating around in the creek. Well, Mom said, "You can tell if they are water proof anyway." The men were called, and they got some horses and pulled the car out.

Irene's Wedding

Irene was going pretty steady with Walter. They were together all the time since Walter worked for Daddy on the farm. Daddy decided it would be good for them not to see each other for a while. Aunt Ethel had surgery, so Irene was sent to help. They teased Walter mercilessly. "It will be cheap to feed Walter tomorrow. Remember when Ruth went to Regina to train for a nurse! The hired hand couldn't eat anything all day, he was so sad!" Well, Walter decided no one would accuse him of that so he ate 7 eggs and a dozen pancakes for breakfast. The separation only strengthened their relationship. When Irene came home Walter quit moping around. His sweetheart had returned.

They would be married soon. Mom didn't feel able to do a bunch of fancy baking, so her sister, Aunt Margaret Lethbridge, came for a couple of weeks. Could she bake good sweets! She whipped up an angel food cake, on a platter with a fork. Yes, you read right, she used a fork to whip the eggs on a platter. The cake was so light and fluffy it just melted in our mouths. One day she made a ginger bread cake. She had brought her twins with her, Wesley and Warren. They asked for a piece of ginger bread. So, Aunt Margaret gave them each some and sent them outside. By now the snow was melting, it was so beautiful. Half an hour later Warren was standing outside still holding his piece. I asked, "What's the matter, don't you like it." He said, "It tastes funny." He was right – it did. She had mistakenly used hot red pepper instead of ginger. It was sure a good thing they tasted it before the wedding. We found out later Earl had switched the labels on the bottles of spices.

Evelyn came for a few days before the wedding to help as well. Carolann was not a year old yet and was walking around in her walker. One day someone forgot and left the cellar door open. Carolann tumbled down the stairs and hit the post that was in the middle of the bottom step. Out came the team of horses and the sleigh and off they dashed to go seven miles through the deep snow to see the doctor. She was fine after they stitched her head up. We were much more careful about keeping the basement door shut after that.

The night before the wedding we had our usual bath night. Evelyn was curling Irene's hair. She did it slowly on purpose because Aunt Margaret was carefully sewing seams all over a bunch of Irene's clothes she was going to pack (to sew them all together). Aunt Margaret folded them up carefully and Irene was so grateful she just packed them and didn't find out Auntie had played a trick on her until she was on her honeymoon.

The day of the wedding all of the neighbours came. The yard was filled with sleighs and the horses were tied up at the corral. That tiny little living room was packed to the doors. In fact, some of the guests had to stand in the kitchen. The minister and Walter stood in one corner of the living room. Irene and cousin Florence came down the narrow stairway from the attic where they had dressed and stood by Walter. The wedding was very short, and I don't remember too much about it except where the minister said – "You can now kiss the bride." When Walter and Irene kissed Grandma McPeek, who sat in the front row, said really loud "huh". Everyone began to laugh.

Out came the food. Actually, I thought the best part was that Mom bought two big jars of dill pickles. Much to Mom's disgust, we girls drank all of the pickle juice in the days that followed the wedding. It was really quite good.

After the wedding was over, Irene and Walter left for Coronach by sleigh where they were to catch a train to Moose Jaw for their honeymoon. The jumper we used to go to school in, was fixed up with a clothes line with diapers hanging on it and lots of decorations.

Soon the wedding was over, and they were off on their honeymoon. Now it was time to milk cows again. Those cows just would never let us forget.

Making A Speech

Every spring we used to have to write an essay or speech. I was so shy and the thought of standing in front of anyone to talk made me sick. Picking a topic was a huge problem. Since Daddy was involved in politics and since they were just trying to implement a health care system Daddy decided this had to be my topic! So, I worked for weeks writing and rewriting, adding to it, editing it. Once it was written I practiced and practiced.

The day finally came to give my speech. The parents all came to school. I guess I wasn't too smart, but I sure tried to do my best. The rest of the kids in the class didn't try too hard because they knew if they won they would have to go to Coronach to give it there. This was where we would compete against other winners in their schools. That was a whole lot more scary. Well, I won first prize, so I had to go to say my speech at the Coronach hall.

The hall was packed with 200 – 300 people. They couldn't all sit down so a lot of people had to stand at the back. The four judges sat in the center in front of the stage with a table and notepads in front of them. There were six of us who went up on the stage and sat in chairs. One at a time we were called to give our speech. Finally, my turn came. I was so scared I thought I would die, but I didn't as you know. I did what Daddy had told me – "Stand up there, take a minute to look around as though everyone owed you $10.00. Then start your talk." So, I did. 300 people owing me $10.00 – Wow! that was a lot of money! I tried to stand tall – a big order for a little girl to do. I looked around, took a deep breath and started to talk. I didn't follow my speech very much - I just talked. When I was finished my speech, I thought the house would explode there was so much applause. I was so relieved when I was done. I don't remember what the other talks were about. Well, I won first prize. There was no money or prize of any kind, just the honour of winning. The local member of parliament, who was there, wanted me to go into politics but I just laughed. I might not be too smart but that didn't even seem to be a very good option for me.

Playing Ball

Once the snow was gone, ball games began. There were only ten kids in our school, and since you need nine players to play ball, we all had to play. I didn't like that at all. That was probably because I was not very good at it. We used to have games with neighbouring schools. Sometimes we played at Mountain Cedar and sometimes at a nearby school. We traveled by horse and wagon, so we missed some school classes - we liked that part.

We also did a lot of practicing long jump, high jumps, broad jumps, racing, etc. The first week in June there was a field day in Coronach. All the little schools around would go in and we were to compete with other kids our age and hopefully come home with a ribbon or two. To start off the day, there was a parade. Each school had a banner they carried and the whole school marched down the streets ending up at the school ground. Once back at the school we were told where to go to compete. The year Uncle Dewey taught us, we had a band. We lead the parade. However, since we were just learning to play they said it was too hard for us to march while we played so they drove us in the back of his big truck. The events were all done by noon and we had picnic lunches. If Mom had any change, we would buy an ice cream or hot dog. The mothers brought lunch and blankets and settled in to have a visit with friends. About 1 p.m. the ball games would start. It was a play off so as a team was eliminated, the winners played against each other. This year we kept winning until the final game. We were to play the town school. I thought, "This is hopeless. The town has all big kids and most of us are little." We were determined to win, but Coronach's team was determined to win too. To do so they cheated and the umpire really favoured them. I can still see Walter screaming his head off at some of the bad calls they made. The 9th inning the score was Coronach 4, Mountain Cedar 5. Coronach was up to bat. This was the end of the 9th inning. There was one on first base, one on second, and one up to bat. They had two out, but if the batter hit a good ball they would win the game. Coronach coach put their strongest player up to bat. Excitement was running high. They were all prepared to celebrate the winning of the trophy as soon as he hit a home run. Our team waited anxiously hoping he would strike out. The ball went hurling over the home base. Whack! He hit it straight to right field where I was standing. They always put me there because I wasn't very good, and balls seldom came out there. I was afraid of the ball. That ball headed straight for me. I've never caught a fly ball in my life, but I thought, "I can always stick my glove up, stop it, then get it and throw it to first". So, I stuck up my hand and everyone started to scream. I didn't know why. Hazel was pounding me on the back. Then I looked down and there was a ball in my glove. We had won the game and won the trophy. The Coronach town school was very angry to be beaten and humiliated by a little country school that had to use all their students, except one little kid, when they had so many big kids on their team to choose from. This was a very sweet victory!

End of School Picnic

School was almost done for the year. We had to study and review our work, then write exams.

After exam time the teacher made us all go to the blackboard where she dictated all our exam marks. We had to write them on the board and add them up to get the average for her. She was lazy so she made us do the work for her. When she would say really low marks we were all scared it was our mark. She didn't call it lazy. She said that we were practicing our math!

Before the end of school, we always planned a picnic. Sometimes we also had a sale of handcrafts we made. For months we would embroider or do wood crafts like cut out flowers, birds or some decoration and make lawn ornaments. Some of the boys didn't work very hard at it. They just saw craft time as a time to goof off. Once again, the money we made went to the Red Cross. We heard so much about the Red Cross during the war that it really meant something to us to help them. The picnic was a great time for all the neighbours to get together. The men gathered in groups talking about farming while the women sat in chairs in the shade or in the school where the crafts were displayed, made coffee and lunch. Later we always ended up gathering around the baseball backstop and watching ballgames. A lot of the kids who had quit school joined in and it became very a competitive game. We did a lot of yelling and screaming and cheering for our favourite team. It was great fun.

We came home with all of our old school books. It was fun to go to the stove and burn the many pages we had laboured over all year. Sometimes we'd have a bonfire in the yard to burn them. We figured we would never need them again since we'd passed on to the next grade.

High School

I took grade nine and ten at Mountain Cedar School, the little one roomed school house where we had gone to school, by correspondence. The teacher helped a little bit but sometimes when she helped it was wrong. Like the time I was learning French. I didn't know that every verb has many forms – she didn't either. So, I thought I was doing very well until the school inspector came. He was French so took a real interest in my work. He about blew his top when he saw my work in "verbs". My teacher got very quiet, and all of a sudden, had an urgent need to teach a lesson to grade three and four students.

Well, finally my grade ten was finished but it was undecided where I would go for grade eleven. Eventually Mom announced that I'd go to Caronport boarding school. At first it was great, but I had a lot of trouble handling the pressure. I didn't know how to handle a class of 40 kids and learn from teachers that just gave lectures. But one class I did enjoy was agriculture. The class was a laugh really. One day the teacher decided he would teach us how to make butter. He proceeded to talk for an hour about taking this many quarts of cream, at this temperature and described the butter churn for about 20 minutes and on and on he went. I just sat there. Why take notes on this? Finally, he noticed I wasn't writing like everyone else. "Shirley, why aren't you taking notes?" he said. "I don't need to cause I've made butter every couple of weeks all my life," I told him. "Well," he retorted, "perhaps, you would like to tell the class." "No," I said, "You are doing quite well." The class just killed themselves with laughter. He turned all red. He cut the lecture short and went on to the next subject.

Then, there was the teacher who made fun of me in class because I was "Scottish." I told him after class that I wasn't "Scottish" but "Irish/German." Well, he made fun of me next class and corrected his previous statement. I was so embarrassed. How unfair it was for him to do that.

I didn't have a lot of good experiences at Carenport. Most of the girls were rich and had a lot of clothes and lots of money to spend. I had no money to buy a treat at the tuck shop. I had to limit the amount of tooth paste I used so that it would last. I had so few clothes and the underarms of my clothes were rotted out by the end of the year.

The food was very poor at Caronport school. Lots of times we just had peanut butter and honey and bread for supper. For a change they served creamed hard cooked eggs on bread or macaroni and cheese. All of this helped most of us to gain weight. I always felt sleep deprived. We had to get up at 6:00 a.m. to be able to get to breakfast on time. It was close to 11:00 p.m. before we got to sleep. I needed way more sleep than that.

The rules were very strict, and we always had a dorm mother spying on us. One of the rules was that we couldn't go to the bathroom during study time. Sometimes we got an urgent call from Mother Nature, so we would sneak down the hall to the large bathroom that 30 of the girls down our hall had to use. We hoped like anything that the dorm mother, Miss Hildebrand, wouldn't catch us. She was merciless when it came to discipline.

Miss Hildebrand also made a rule that all girls had to wear nylon stockings until she deemed that it was warm enough for bobby socks. This is where the rich kids indirectly helped me out. My nylons were full of holes and I didn't have the money to buy new ones. The rich girls had fancy bobby socks and wanted to wear them. In protest they wore the holiest nylons they could find. If theirs didn't have enough holes they would make some. Mine looked good in comparison. Unfortunately, it didn't make any difference to Miss Hildebrand. In fact, she waited longer before she allowed us to wear bobby socks for spite.

We also had gratis work to do two or three hours during the day. The students did much of the work done at the school. The gratis work was considered as part of the tuition. Our jobs were setting tables, clearing tables, washing dishes, peeling potatoes, scrubbing floors, cleaning bathrooms, cleaning the dorm halls and entrances, laundry duty – on and on the list went. Some jobs were more desirable than others, but all took 2 - 3 hours each day.

I got so homesick. One winter night I remember hanging my head out the window with tears streaming down my face. It was a beautiful star light night. Snow was sparkling under the stars and crunched under the feet of passersby. There was a team of horses jogging down the street pulling a sleigh. The harnesses jingled. What I would have given to have gone for a ride.

Princess Elizabeth came to Moose Jaw that year. All the rich kids had money to go see her. I didn't have any money, so I sat in my room and saw her train all lit up and snaking its way across the dark landscape. It was all lit up like fairyland. Even if I didn't get to see my princess, I consoled myself that I saw her train. It was so awesome! Later that year her father died, and she became our queen.

Well, finally the school year was over, and I got to go home. How good it felt! I was so grateful to find that Daddy was going to drive us to the Coronach school the following year. They had closed the Mountain Cedar School.

Grade 12 was uneventful. There were only four of us in grade 12 at Coronach High School. One day I was the only one in class. Mr. Aldous decided we would do an experiment. We would make H$_2$S (hydrogen sulfide) gas. Since it would be smelly, we would do the experiment outside on the front step of the school. When we came back in, of course some of the smell came too. The Grade 11 boys all said, "Shirley what did you do?" How embarrassed I was!

One time, Mr. Aldous decided we would dissect an earthworm. Now, worms and I just do not mix! Not at all! He laid the pickled earthworm on a paper towel and got the other three students to rub their finger over it, so they could feel its legs before he cut it open. When I didn't do it, he took my hand and tried to force me to touch it. I screamed so loudly that I disrupted the whole school. He got the idea that I wasn't going to touch this creature and gave up trying to make me.

I had many an argument in class with Mr. Aldous. He knew that I was a Christian. I think there were only two Christians in the whole room and he taunted me for it. He could say what he wanted about me and I would not talk back. Attack my Christian faith, and I stood up to him and would not back down. He finally gave up and quit bugging me.

We planned a long time for our graduation. I drew a dress design of my dream dress. It was everything I could possibly want in a dress. Three weeks before graduation Mom and Ruth went to the city. They brought home an ugly dress for me to wear. I didn't complain, because I knew money was short. I didn't say too much because I didn't want to hurt their feelings, but I was terribly disappointed. Ruth made some changes to the dress so that it wasn't quite as bad to look at. I was stuck wearing it. It's only saving grace was that it was floor length.

The week of graduation it started to rain. It poured steadily for three days straight. The roads between our farm and the highway were dirt. When it rained heavily, they turned into 3 miles of deep mud. Mom kept saying, "Well, I guess we can't go." I just stood looking out the window – looking up the road with tears in my eyes. I was not wanting to be deprived of the one special event in my life, so I got ready to go and waited. Finally, Walt and Dad came in to the house. Walt, my brother-in-law said, "Dad you go ahead to the highway in the truck and I'll follow you with the tractor in case you get stuck.

Dad and Mom really didn't care if they went to my graduation, to them it was a lot of fuss over nothing. And they sure didn't want to venture out in the mud to get there.

However, since they saw how set I was on going, they finally gave in and got ready to go. Off we went slipping and sliding in the mud with Walter following on the tractor. Finally, we reached the highway where the road was paved. From there into town it was easy driving.

We reached town in time for the banquet and I made it to my graduation. It wasn't a very fancy affair, but it was special to me. I was always so grateful to Walter for making it possible for me to get there.

The Armour

Buy the truth and sell it not.
There are battles to be fought.
Put the breast plate on for sure
And the battle you'll endure.

Shod your feet with the gospel of peace
Be assured the battle won't cease
Quench the darts of the wicked one
With the shield of faith in God's only Son.

———

"So teach us to number our days that we might apply our heart to wisdom." Psalm 90:12

Church

Mom taught us from the Bible but for a few years there was no church or Sunday school. Finally, Merle Noble, a neighbor about Evelyn's age, and Daddy decided to start a Sunday school in our Mountain Cedar school. Sunday school was usually held in the late morning, so we had time to do chores and clean up. [Sunday mornings, I was usually in charge of polishing all the shoes after helping to milk the cows.]

Merle lead the Sunday school and taught the adults and Evelyn taught the kids. There were so many of us in our family that we were about half of the group whenever we got together. Soon neighbors began to come. More and more came. Soon Sunday school was extended to include a church service. Merle did the preaching and Daddy always had his fiddle. He always made that old fiddle almost say the words. It was so beautiful. Attendance grew, and it was finally decided to move the church to Coronach.

After church we always had a nice dinner when we got home. Often chicken and pie. We did a lot of baking on Saturday. I usually made the pies. I liked to make pies, but I didn't like to clean the chickens. Oh, what a yucky job to put a hand in and pull out the innards of the chicken.

The Pressure Cooker

Daddy loved to spend money and Mom was always trying to find ways to save money. One day Daddy came home from town with a big shiny pressure cooker. Daddy gave Mom a list of all the virtues of the cooker to convince her that it was money well spent, but Mom was very upset. She just gave Daddy the silent treatment. Finally, he gave up. "Well," he said, "The store-keeper said you could try it out and if you didn't like it he would take it back." Then he went out to work. Mom did a lot of thinking and came up with a plan. She was going to prove that the cooker was no good! "Girls," she said, "Go out and catch that old rooster and kill it." Now the rooster was about five years old and would be too tough to eat. He had gotten away when the rest of the chickens were butchered, and Mom thought he had earned the right to live. He had lived on and on for five years. We caught him and got him ready to cook. The next morning Mom did as she often did – she cut the rooster into pieces, rolled the pieces in flour, and browned them. Then she laid them in the cooker ready to cook. She was sure that the old rooster would be far too tough to eat so she put a roast on to cook too so that we wouldn't go hungry. When the old rooster was finally cooked I can still hear her say, "Well, I do declare. This chicken is so tender it is like a young chicken!" Daddy had won the argument, and Mom had lost. We had pressure cooker chicken and stew many, many times over the years.

Over the years Mom's hands got more swollen, and sore. Sometimes there were things she could not do because of it. One thing she found hard was closing the pressure cooker. She would get it started to cook and when one of us would walk by she would get us to twist it closed. That way she got the cooker started sooner than if she had to wait for someone to come in. One day she forgot it wasn't closed tight and let the pressure build up. All of a sudden, she heard a boom. The pressure had built up and the cooker exploded the lid off. What a mess! Chicken was all over the stove. The lid had flown up and hit the warming oven door, which was open and put a big dent in it. We were very thankful Mom had just gone over to the other side of the room, so she wasn't hurt. After that she was very nervous about using the pressure cooker.

This Wonderful Salvation

This wonderful plan of Salvation
The redemption for mankind
This wonderful gift of Salvation
No better gift can you find

The Lord Jesus came to save
Oh what a wondrous plan
To save the little lost ones
Picture it if you can.

He also came to seek those
Who are lost and deep in sin
He longs to come to set you free
And live your heart within.

He offers you forgiveness
No matter what you've done
He offers you salvation
Through God's beloved son.

Oh won't you trust the Saviour
Jesus – God's only son
T'is a wonderful gift of salvation
Oh trust this Beloved One!

Summer Bible School

In the summer Evelyn always planned a summer Bible school. This was again a gospel outreach. It was held in the neighbouring school. Evelyn arranged to have a couple of ladies come from the City to help her. An invitation went out to the whole community. Kids that were too far away to come each day stayed overnight at our house. Evelyn and her helpers stayed in the attic. The rest of us kids, and neighbour kids, spread our blankets on the floor in the living room. It was wall-to-wall kids.

At Bible school we had some really neat crafts to do and learned some new songs and stories. At the end of the week we put on a program for the parents and showed off our crafts and some of the things we had learned. Then, of course, there was the coffee and cakes. This outreach was a way to get the gospel into homes of neighbours, who would not come to church.

OH YES

Yes, I have words as you shall see
Of One who died upon the tree.
For all my sins which were excess
So many words just can't express.

Though I would tell it all day long
Express it in an all-day song
I wouldn't even begin to say
How glad I am they're washed away.

He came, a child in manger born
But many, many laugh and scorn
He died upon a cross for me,
For ever I will thankful be.

A Visiting Preacher

One fall (I think that I was 11 or 12), a visiting speaker came along. It was decided to hold a gospel meeting at East Polar School. Daddy got out his truck (it had high sides on the box) and we all piled in. It was a 30-minute drive, so we all fastened our kerchiefs on our heads, so the wind wouldn't mess our hair too much, and off we went. The room was packed. We sat in the desks like school kids and there were a few benches at the back. The rest of the people just stood. I don't remember what the speaker spoke about. I didn't listen too much. I studied the ceiling, counted lights, counted people, anything to keep my mind occupied so I didn't have to listen. I didn't like to hear about being a sinner. Of course, I didn't think that I was one anyway. I didn't drink, smoke or go to dances. At the end of his message, he started to ask if anyone wanted to have their sins washed away. I thought, "I'm pretty good. I go to Sunday school. I don't lie or steal." Then a strange thing happened. My big brother, Bud, went to the front and kneeled down. "Wow!" I thought. "He is almost perfect! So, if he needs it I sure do." Then I started to realize how much a sinner I really was. I accepted the Lord as my Saviour that day. Oh, it was so great! On the way home (there must have been 15 or more of us in the back of the truck) we sang hymns at the top of our lungs. Since then, I haven't always walked with the Lord as I should, but I can honestly say the Lord has been King of my life. He has helped me through many a hard time.

A Little Child

As a little child I was always taught
There are many battles to be fought.

Since Jesus died upon the tree
He is there for you and me.

On the cross His blood He shed
This is what the Bible said.

All have sinned the Bible reads
That means me I must concede!

But I was good I did not go
To the dance or the show.

Telling lies I did not do
Saying only what was true.

That was great for the bad you see
But it surely wasn't meant for me.

Then one night the preacher came
He would preach in Jesus name.

So into the truck we all piled in
To hear how Jesus died for sin.

The preacher preached so earnestly
I counted lights complacently.

I counted desks and saw who came
I knew them all, yes all by name.

The preacher preached for oh so long
Then he ended with a song.

Then he said something to my surprise
"I'm going to pray, don't open your eyes."

"Thank you, God for sending your Son
To this world for the sinful one."

"To this world to die on the tree
For all the sinner's like you and me."

I thought it was over but to my surprise
He quietly said, "Don't open your eyes."

"I want you to think while the music plays
Do you want to do what the Bible says."

"Then come to the front, kneel on your knees
And listen to the Saviour's pleas."

"He'll wash away your dirty sins
So then in heaven you may enter in."

That's great for the bad you see
But it certainly wasn't meant for me.

For I was good, I didn't go
To the dance or the show.

Telling lies I did not do
Saying only what was true.

That was great for the bad you see
But it surely wasn't meant for me.

Then all of a sudden, I got quite a shock
For down the aisle my brother did walk.

My eyes flew open, open so wide
Was he a sinner for whom Jesus died?

He was my brother, near perfect you see
If he needed Jesus then what about me?

I know then for certain, as certain can be
It was for me that Jesus died on the tree.

I accepted the Saviour right there on the spot
And knew then for certain, salvation I got.

My sins, Oh so many, He knew everyone
He washed them away with the blood of His Son.

Many a lesson I've learned you see
But the best I have learned at my Mother's knee.

WHAT A GIFT

Jesus for all mans' sins did die
His blood was shed for me
And He again went up on high
So eternal life I'd see.

Oh Lord my heart I give to Thee
I long to look above
Thy presence Lord oh let me see
Oh, fill me with thy love.

To serve Thee with my life I fail
To live the way I should
Oh, help me Lord for Thee to hail
Lord of my life I would.

Into your heart ask Him today
His blood cleanses from sin
And you will be His child always
He'll give you peace within

One day He's coming bye and bye
For all His ransomed throng
To take us with Him up on high
I pray it won't be long.

———

My big sister, Evelyn, was always very active in Sunday school and church activities. She always thought we should have a Sunday School Christmas concert. One year, Evelyn decided to have the Christmas concert at our house. We all spent hours practicing – singing, poems and of course the story of the birth of Christ. Evelyn organized the house cleaning too. For weeks we washed and waxed the floors until they shone. Daddy kept saying – "Why do you fuss? When it is over you'll never know you had it looking like this." But Evelyn insisted that we need it all shiny and clean. The evening of the concert the living room was packed. There was not a square inch that wasn't used for seating guests.

Mom's bedroom was the stage – the large arch with curtains for a door made it perfect. We dressed in our costumes in the attic and stood in the stairway when we weren't on stage. Mom made us some brand-new flannelette nightgowns that were perfect for angel costumes. Our grey wool blankets from the woollen mills were put over shoulders for shepherds. It was so much fun! The program was short but well planned out. When it was finished, Sunday school prizes and candy bags were handed out. Then we had coffee and the cakes that we had been baking for weeks. Once it was over, and our guests were gone, we swept up. There were peanut shells, orange peels and wrapping paper in abundance. It was a very rewarding evening. The best thing of all was that the story of Jesus was told to numerous unsaved neighbours!

Our Family

An interesting family
We have – I am sure.
3 Boys and 6 girls
Our love will endure

We had wonderful parents
Who worked very hard
To feed us and guide us
they're now with the Lord.

The love that they showed us
We have to this day,
Since many an hour
For us they did pray.

"We can't tell you apart,
Like peas in a pod
You all look alike"
One was heard to applaud.

We all are alike
Yet different for sure,
Each has his own place
in this family so dear.

Grace Evelyn the eldest
Her short life she lived
A wonderful example
Of how we should live.

Then there was Ruth
Kind hearted indeed.
Always ready and willing
To help others in need.

Bud our first brother
So gentle and kind.
Is the best kind of brother,
you ever could find.

Irene then comes next
So quiet serene.
A sister to be proud of
Is what I do mean.

Hazel was always
A companion and friend.
I love her with love
That never can end.

Then I come next
In the family tree.
So thankful to be part
Of this family.

Earl our next brother,
Kind hearted and true.
A very great brother
I can now assure you.

Then George came along
So proud were we all.
Now he works with the Indians
He answered God's call.

Last there was Linda
She can sing and oh how.
We love her so much
I can tell you right now.

We know how God blessed us
and we feel very sure,
We have a great love
Which will always endure.

———

Country Girl in the Big City

After graduation I started to think, "What next?" The only options I had were – secretary, teacher or nurse. None of these appealed to me. I didn't think I was smart enough to go to University, so I spent weeks getting things ready to go to the city in search of a job.

For days I collected things to take. First, of course, I collected the few clothes that I had. Then Mom gave me a couple of blankets, a sheet, pillowcase and pillow, a couple towels, tea towels and a few dishes and cooking pots. Finally, I was all packed and ready to go. Hazel would join me for six weeks while she took summer school. Then I would be on my own.

Mom tried to get the Alliance minister, in Regina, to help us get located but he wasn't interested. So, it was decided we would rent a room the first night from Canadian Bible Institute since school was out until fall.

Walt drove us to Regina. He couldn't find a place to park so stopped long enough at the curb for us to drag our trunk out of the truck, and then headed home.

Here we were – two young girls and a big trunk to drag across the street in rush hour traffic. To make matters worse I didn't know how the lights worked. I knew red meant stop, green meant go. I had learned that by listening to the grades one and two as they read their new readers. But stop and consider – on one corner there are two red lights and two green lights, which one do you obey? It was a big question for a little country girl that had never seen them before.

Well, we finally braved the traffic and dragged our trunk across through the busy street to the Bible school and arranged a room. Then we went in search of a bite to eat and a newspaper, so we could look for a place to live. We finally found a tiny attic room. It was clean, but the water pipes were so corroded that we had trouble getting enough water to wash our face let alone enough for a bath. This was home for the next few months.

Hazel went off to school, and I went downtown to look for a job. I thought working in a store would be fun. Little did I know how awful it would be. I walked bravely into Kresgies 5 & 10 cent store and asked where the office was. Up some rickety, dark, dirty stairs, I found myself in a cluttered office. The girl behind the desk shoved a form over for me to fill in. I did this for her and sat and waited. There were several other girls there and I was so afraid that they would get hired instead of me. After long hours anxiously waiting in the tiny stuffy office, a man came in and asked if I could start the next day. I was elated and decided to stop for a real treat on the way home. I stopped at a coffee shop and spent some of my precious little money for a coffee and a piece of pie because now I had a job! I was about to make my fortune.

Work was very hard. I was on my feet all day long. I had to wait on customers, keep the counters all neatly arranged and worst of all I had to go into the crowded, dark basement to get new products to keep the counters full as I sold things to customers. To get to the basement I went down steep, narrow, dirty stairs. At the bottom of the stairs the whole floor was covered from floor to ceiling with shelves, leaving only narrow little aisles between. I couldn't reach most of the shelves, so I had to climb the shelves to reach. Empty boxes filled the aisle almost waist deep. With my short legs, it was almost impossible to negotiate through them – especially when I had a load of product boxes to carry up the stairs. It wasn't long before my feet got so sore from walking on cement all day in poor fitting shoes that I could hardly bear it. I went home most nights too tired to eat.

By the end of the summer I found that my meagre wage barely covered the rent and a wee bit of food. I ate a lot of peanut butter sandwiches. Often it was all I could afford. It was not the fortune that I expected.

I knew there must be a better job that I could get. One day I met a young man who worked for Saskatchewan Telephone Co. "Why don't you go and apply there," he said, "I will recommend you." So off I marched on my lunch hour to apply. A few days later I got a call saying that I had gotten the job. I was delighted. It was a little bit better pay (Instead of $26 a week, I was making $35 a week) and a whole lot easier work. I worked there until a few months after I was married three years later.

Vacation

We only ever went on one family vacation. Daddy was quite content to just stay home. If he had any spare time, he spent it reading his novels. He didn't even like to picnic. Of course, he could not object to school or Sunday school picnics, but a couple times we tried to set up a table outside in the shade when it was too hot inside to eat. When Daddy came home he asked, "Why do we have a house if we couldn't eat in it?" and made us carry it all in before he would eat.

Once after I had been working a full year, Hazel and I came home and proposed a family vacation. My friend, Vivian, and her family were going to the hot springs at Saco Montana. We would like to join them there for a few days. To our surprise Daddy agreed. So, we hurriedly packed a few clothes and cooking supplies and off we went. It seemed like it took forever to get there as we bumped along in the old pickup with the makeshift camper on the back. In reality, it was only about 30 miles, but it seemed like a thousand.

At the resort the water was great, but as soon as we got out of it, we thought we would fry. It was about 110°F and no wind. There was not a tree to be seen and very little grass. The ground was dry and as flat as a pancake. This didn't dampen our spirits at all. We swam and played in the water all day long, stopping only long enough to fix a quick bite to eat then headed back to the pool. Mom and Mrs. Torgerson found a nice shallow bit of water in the shade of the building and visited and relaxed. Dad found a shady spot to read. I think this was the first time Mom ever took so much time to relax and she really enjoyed it.

By the end of the second day we looked like red tomatoes – blisters on top of blisters. At the end of the fourth day Daddy had had enough, so we packed up and headed home. It was a wonderful vacation.

———

Over the next two years I rented a lot of different rooms. Some were so scary I had to move. One was a third-floor room where the landlord was a little wrinkled man of foreign descent. I didn't worry too much about him until one day I was in the basement washing my clothes. He insisted he wanted to help me. He grabbed my pile of clothes and started to sort my underwear. I freaked out and ran up to my room. Then, I watched to see if he had to leave the house for some reason. When he went out for a few minutes I ran down, grabbed my clothes and ran back to my room as fast as I could. I barely missed him as he came back in. From then on, I washed clothes by hand and hung them in my room. I found another place to live as soon as I could.

One house where I lived, they made us have all of our things fumigated. They said that this was to prevent us from bringing in bed bugs. The room was tiny with a table in one corner with a hot plate on it. This was our kitchen. One other corner we put a couch that folded up so that we could walk around it in the daytime. They were very strict there. We had to be quiet by 9:00 p.m. and after 9:30 we had to whisper, or they would bang on the door and threaten to evict us. Rooms were very hard to find so we whispered.

One time the place I lived in was on a street that was not well lit. I was walking down this little, dark, tree-lined street and worried as I passed each bush that someone would jump out and grab me. I heard footsteps behind me. I sped up. The footsteps sped up. Finally, they caught up to me. By this time my heart was in my mouth. Then I heard a high-pitched little voice say, "Can I walk with you? I'm scared." It was a girl that lived two doors down from me. We both relaxed and continued on home.

Many scary things happened to me. Most of which I do not wish to re-live, they are too painful. All I can say is, the Lord is good! He kept me safe! He knew I was a little country girl that did not know the ways and evils of the big bad world I had come to live in.

One day, the girl in the room across the hall from me said, "I have found a room to move to, but can't afford it. Would you share it with me? I agreed and to my surprise it turned out to be a Christian couple – Norman and Gertie Clark. "Aunt Gertie" became a second mother to me. We had a lot of fun while living at Aunt Gertie's. Hazel moved in. Our room was about 12 feet square but had a veranda that we could use in the summer. As soon as the snow began to melt we opened the door and it was a wonderful addition. When summer came and Hazel's friend Freida came for the summer while going to summer school. My friend Evelyn moved into another room next door so it was a party all of the time. Every week we got together for supper one night. We each took turns hosting supper but we all brought food. I am sure sometimes other people who lived close by wondered what was so funny because we did so much laughing. It was so great to have such good friends.

———

Norman and Gertie took me to the Assembly where I met Alan in 1955. After the first date we both knew that God wanted us to be together. We had many happy times together during the next ten months.

———

February 29th was called Sadie Hawkins day. This was the one day where it was acceptable for a girl to ask a man out on a date. Any other day it was considered rude and too bold to do so. I called Al and asked him out to dinner. When he arrived at our house, I had a corsage waiting for him – a big corsage – which was made with green onion, radishes, and other vegetables. It was really quite pretty, but oh so smelly. I pinned it on Al, but soon he took it off again. It smelled so bad that he couldn't stand it. Oh well, it was good for some more laughter. We went out for supper anyway and had a great time.

One day I came downstairs and stopped in the living room door. There was Aunt Gertie sitting on a stool by the fireplace – her favorite place to sit. She was eating peanuts and the shells were spilling onto the floor a few at a time. She offered me some. Such a little old lady. So sweet and gentle. I did the unthinkable. I walked over to her and took a handful and dropped them onto her lap and said, "Nuts to the monkey" and took off up the stairs as fast as I could. Can you believe this little frail old lady had me down and was sitting on me before I got up 3 steps. I was so shocked. She wouldn't let me up until I said that I was sorry.

We often sat around her fireplace and chatted. When Al came to see me he joined us. There was many a wonderful evening we spent there. One night as we sat around, Aunt Gertie brought a tray of glasses filled with apple juice. As we sipped, her bird, Lizzy, was flying around and seeming to be very interested in all of the activity. When she saw the glasses she was fascinated and settled down on Al's glass and took a drink. "Ok, Lizzy, have some. It is so good." Lizzy took a few drinks, then a few more. Then she decided to fly to the top of the door where she often sat observing the activities of the room. Well, she couldn't make it up to the top of the door. After many tries, she finally caught her toes in the lace curtain on the door and scrambled up. She finally made it to the top and proceeded to try to walk down the door. She looked like a drunk trying to walk the straight line for the police. We laughed until we cried while Aunt Gertie scolded Al, in no uncertain terms, for getting her bird drunk.

———————

Spring went by quickly and soon we were preparing for our wedding. We were married on August 4, 1956, in Coronach in the church that I had grown up in. My school teacher, Mrs. Henderson came to our wedding. She said that she had now attended all of her students' weddings.

(*Christine, Hazel, Shirley, Alan, Jack, Earl*

In front - Cheryl, Gordon)

It was the hottest day of the summer. Dad Heslop loaned us his car to go on a honeymoon to the Black Hills of North Dakota. It was a yellow and black and kids wanted to write with lipstick on the car. Mom Heslop stood by the car and guarded it. No one was going to write on her car. Somehow a few things did get written on it with white shoe polish. It baked on and sure was hard to remove but did no damage.

Al's brother, Jack, and my brother, Earl, my sister Hazel, and cousin, Christine, stood up with us. My nephew Doug was to be the ring bearer and niece Cheryl was my flower girl. At the last minute, Doug wouldn't go down the aisle, so my nephew Gordon walked instead. Lunch was served in the basement of the church by the local church ladies. It was all very nice, but by the time the wedding was over and pictures taken by the white church which reflected so much bright light, Al had gotten a nasty, nasty headache and he was sick all night.

As we left the church, Al's friends from Regina followed us, thinking they were bugging us. We really didn't care and were thankful they were with us when we came to cross the border in to the USA. Dad Heslop had some USA tires on the car so someone had to crawl under to get serial numbers off of them. His friend Warren did that. We spent a wonderful week in the Black Hills. It was the second holiday I had ever had so I particularly enjoyed it.

Epilogue

We came back to Regina and settled into an attic apartment. The bathroom was on the second floor and all was well until I started to get morning sickness. Every time someone would start to cook, the smell came directly up the stairs. Then one day Al went hunting and came home with a duck. I had no idea how to cook it, but I cleaned it and put it in salt water to see if it would take some of the wild taste away. Then the phone rang. Would we like to go to the country for the weekend? Of course, we would. So away we went – no more thoughts of the duck sitting in salt water. When we came home Sunday night we were met with a nasty smell. Really nasty. I lifted the pot lid and met with the source and immediately started to throw up. Al took the whole pot and all to the garbage and dumped it in. So – I didn't have to cook a duck after all. By this time I knew that I was pregnant and we needed a better place to live. We found a little basement suite which was so perfect. Kenn was born May 9, 1957 – weighing in at 10 lbs 7 oz and 23 inches tall.

We were still living in a little basement suite. Three years later when Hope arrived March 16, 1960. Soon after that we were able to buy a small house. What a treat to be in our own home and not have to worry about a landlord. Alan was now working for Esso. He started as a draftsman and had advanced to working in the engineering department. We had a large garden in the back yard and were able to grow a lot of our food.

Family photo taken after Daddy's funeral in 1963

front row: Linda, Irene, Ruth, Mom, Evelyn, Hazel, Shirley

back row: George, Walter (Irene), Don (Ruth), Thelma (Bud), Bud, Irene (Earl), Earl, Ed (Hazel), Art (Evelyn), Alan (Shirley)

We were interested in helping the young people, so we started a youth group in our home and for six years we held young people's meetings every week. It was a real privilege to watch the kids grow as they learned the Word of God.

Glenn arrived March 7, 1968. Now we had three wonderful children. How blessed we were!

Alan was now spending more and more time working in Calgary. Finally, he was transferred there and on July 1, 1969 we all moved there. It was a big city. I said, "I would never drive my car here." But we had only been there a few weeks when things changed. Alan had been out supervising work at an oil rig and came home at six am. He would take the day off. It wasn't to happen though. Soon the boss called, and said it didn't matter if he had not slept for 36 hours. He was needed. He drove in to the office and handed me the keys and told me to go home. So, I did what I had to do and managed just fine.

Alan worked for Esso for 21 years then decided to start his own consulting company and **Coment** was born. We had a computer that was the size of a fridge and a dish washer together. It had to be in an air-conditioned room. Al was still working at Esso when we started it, so it was me who had to find an office space and arrange the renovations and for the telephone lines to be installed and bought furniture, etc. There were a lot of things that I had to do.

All was well, until the government put in the national energy policy which killed the oil industry. We were able to sell the company to a man and work for him. Now we had an income again.

Eventually we bought a small farm at Irricana, Alberta, by now and were looking for a way to make money there. We discovered ostriches. Soon we were on our way to Oklahoma to pick some up. For eight years we raised ostriches. We had a lot of fun but lost a lot of money was well. Finally, the ostrich industry collapsed. Most of the birds that we had were being boarded for other folks and the folks quit paying.

About this time, I had a head-on collision and was hurt badly, and soon after that Al was diagnosed with prostate cancer. That winter was very cold, and we had piles of snow. The birds had to be kept inside because of the cold. Many of the birds died. It was very discouraging. Alan had massive radiation treatments. Doctors told us later they didn't expect him to live through it. He was very weak, but for five years he was cancer free. Finances were very bad, so we sold our farm and moved to Airdrie, Alberta.

Al got some oil industry consulting work. The Lord had provided an income for us again. After several years it proved profitable enough we were able to, with Glenn's help, start to build homes to rent. I worked alongside of Glenn all day, and when he went home to his family, Al came home from work and we worked until late at night finishing the interior of the houses. I learned how to use a water pump and walk around in heavy mud and drain ponds that were in the foundations of where the houses were to be built. Also, I learned how to lay ceramic tile and most of all I learned supervise building trades without fear.

Five years later Al's cancer came back. He now is on hormone shots to slow it down. I had been working very hard and decided to slow down. While sitting at my computer, I had a stroke. It just affected my speech and made me very dizzy. Twice now I have had to learn to speak again, but the Lord is good and I am back to normal again.

We bought a 42 foot yacht and decided to take some time off and spent several winters in Florida. It was wonderful to be out of the cold for the winters. However, Al continued to feel more tired and his hip was very sore. He couldn't get down to do the maintenance of the boat. We had to put her up for sale.

Now we are settled here in Airdrie and trust the Lord for what He has in store for us in the future. I don't know what the future holds, but we know Who holds the future. That is good enough for me to rest in!

We have been married for 63 years now. We are more in love each day. Over the years we've seen many hard times, but many joys too. Each trial and hardship the Lord has seen us through. Each joyous occasion was like the sun coming out in all of its splendour after a rain.

The Lord has blessed us with three children – Kenneth Alan, Hope Candace and Glenn Andrew. He has also given us one son-in-law – Brian - and two daughters-in-law - Lois and Angela. We have given thanks to the Lord many times for our children. The Lord added another blessing for us when He gave us special grandchildren – Daniel, Elisabeth, John, Rebecca, Sarah, David, Jacqueline, Benjamin, Cassi, Annisa, Michell, Spencer and Max. We also have 5 Great Grandchildren - Janica, Clara, Neil, Caleb and Abigail.

My Poems

Poetry written over the years for memorable events in my life.

Our Sister Ruth

(Written in the car on the way to her funeral)

Ruth was our loving sister and friend.
Grandmother and wonderful mother.
Like Lydia of old she worked with her hands
And toiled for the good of another.

She entertained and cared for their needs
She cooked, and she sewed and did mend.
She handcrafted quilts a real work of art
And often a hand she did lend.

Her life here on earth though not really long
Was ever so wrought with pain
How much we don't know for it didn't show
But you never heard her complain.

I'm sure she wanted her life to have counted
And bring comfort and joy to others
A great example to follow for sure
For children and sisters and brothers.

The memories we have we'll treasure forever
But she wanted us not to forget
Her Saviour and Lord who carried her through
And all her needs here He met.

And now He has said – your work here is done
Your journey here on earth will end.
And now He has lovingly and quietly come
And carefully carried her home.

So, let us thank Him for all he has done
For strength for the road ahead
For strength and wisdom and comfort and love
For all the memories we have.

I imagine what she would say if I could talk to her now
"Remember me, sure, but make much of Christ."
What think ye of Christ?
He is altogether lovely!

John

*(Glenn's best friend was like a son to us. He was killed when he
rolled our truck while he lived with us on the farm.)*

We miss you John.
Just two short weeks ago,
You shared our home, our lives.
We wish you could have stayed.

We miss you John.
So quickly snatched away.
No more to laugh and love and work.
The way you used to do.

We miss you John.
Your laughing deep blue eyes.
They told of deep deep feelings.
They sparkled as you talked.

We miss you John.
Your blond hair neatly combed.
To show a lock of hair
Beneath your Stetson brim.

We miss you John.
The boy who loved to dress,
With your wranglers neatly worn
Your boots and belt and hat.

We miss you John.
Your noisy boisterous ways.
You'd come bursting in the room
"Hi, How are you doing Eh?"

We miss you John.
With your gentle caring ways.
Your thoughtful living manner
You every day displayed.

We miss you John.
One coffee drinking friend.
You learned to go without your cream
For cowboys drink it black.

We miss you John.
You talked and talked some more.
Of things in distant ages
The way they used to be.

We miss your John.
If you could talk today
What would you now be saying
But our dear Saviour's praise.

We miss you John.
But soon will come the day
When we will quickly join you
To meet the Lord up there.

We miss you John
You're with the Saviour now.
May we in some small measure
Share the joy you have today.

We miss you John
But my earnest prayer today
Is that I might live each day
As if it were the last.

"So teach us to number our days that we might apply our heart to wisdom." Psalm 90:12

I Must Go

(*Written when I had a stroke and thought that I was going to die***)**

When He calls me, I must go
He has said, "It will be so!"

No more worry, no more pain
Oh, just think, no not again!

No more work, no more strife
I'm all done here – with battles of life

No more sickness, no more sorrow,
Only promised, a bright tomorrow

No more trudging down life's long lane
No more diets or weight to gain!

No more wanting Que cards from above
But basking in the Saviour's love

Don't weep for me – Oh perhaps a bit
As at your table I no longer sit

I have loved you – Oh so much!
May you feel the Saviour's touch

May He comfort, give you a song
This is His way, it can't be wrong

My work is o'er, my work is done
Now live with His beloved Son

I've just gone on, gone on before
My Blessed Saviour to adore

I'll wait for you, it won't be long
We'll all be singing heaven's song

We'll sing and praise and shout with glee
"We'll spend eternity with Thee!"

Oh what bliss, what joy 'twill be
To gaze upon His face to see

The story of Esther

Our Kids loved it when we were
traveling and we would read the whole book of Esther while
driving down the highway. God Takes Care of His Own

The kings was so restless
He could not sleep
He tossed all night
Perhaps counting sheep.

Bring me the books
Of records you keep.
Perhaps if I read
It will help me to sleep.

He read and he read
Right there on his bed.
How some wicked men
Had wanted him dead.

They hatched out a plan
T'was so absurd.
"We will kill the King."
But Mordecai heard.

He made hast to tell
Make known to the King.
That these wicked men
Planned death to him bring.

What great has been done
To honour this man.
Who endangered his life
To thwart their great plan.

Oh – nothing was done
You just look and read
Nothing was done
That was not decreed.

Just then came a knock
A knock at the door.
Haman stuck out his chest
For all to adore.

He came there so boldly
He came with a request.
To kill all the Jews.
From the east to the west.

What can I do now
Please tell me young man.
An honour that's due
To a brave faithful man.

Now Haman so thought
As he so often did.
Who would he honour
More than this grownup kid.

So he stuck out his chest
In proud joyful glee.
"Put on him your coat
So all man can see."

"Let him ride on your horse
As it's lead through the streets."
"Shouting get on your knees

Get off your feet."
Will you honour this man
Tis the king's own decree.
Now Haman so thought
He is thinking of me.

The king then spoke
His voice was quite stern.
Go take Mordecai now
No delays my concern.

So proud Haman went
His head held so low.
Led him down the street
He watched people bow.

Queen Esther had a party
Two she did invite.
Haman and the king
To the banquet that night.

Now Haman was happy
"I'm special" says he.
"None were invited
But little old me."

They ate, and they feasted
And partied all night.
And all the great food
T'was an awesome sight.

The king then spoke up
And asked of the queen.
"I want to please you

For this I am keen."
"Whatever you wish
I'll give you and more.
Tell me now Esther
The queen I adore"

"Oh king I must tell you
I'm sure you need to know.
An evil plan is hatching
I assure you its so."

"To kill all my people
Is the wicked plan.
I'm sorry to tell you
That Haman is the man."

Oh Haman was frightened.
As frightened can be
The King was so angry
T'was very plain to see.

"My Queen you'll not trouble
You rogue, wicked one
You'll hang on the gallows
Before the day's done."

Contemplation

A soft wind blows the gentle breeze
Over the land and open seas.

Soft clouds drift so lazily by
In the soft blue summer's sky.

The grasses wave and toss their heads
The roses bloom in the flower beds.

Little waves dance on the reflective creek
Mother duck catches a bug in her beak.

Her babies follow her, yes all five
Saying it's great to be alive.

Along the creek runs a much used trail
Children on skateboards and women frail.

Children and young people, old ones too
People with dogs in the morning dew.

I sit on my deck as they go by
Watching the plane high up in the sky.

Kids with kites that go bobbing around
Even a dinosaur makes no sound.

The boy holds on with all his might
While the wind tugs it almost out of sight.

And the robin sits in the top of a tree

The flower is kissed by the bumble bee.

All this I see as I sit on my chair
I sit and relax and breath the fresh air.

I can't help but wonder, my contemplation is
How much He must love us to give me all this!

A Summer Storm

The day is hot the sun shines bright
Fans are working with all their might
To cool the stifling air.

Children are playing in their bathing suits
They've kicked off their shoes and kicked off their boots
To dance in the sprinkler cool.

The old men sit out of the blazing sun,
Women talk of the work to be done.
But it's too hot to really care.

Small babies cry because they're too hot
But they must sleep like it or not.
For babies need their sleeping

Mothers plan supper on the Bar-BQ
They must try it out because it is new,
And cook cook while sitting on the deck.

Out of the west the storm clouds roll
Angry and black and out of control
Warning of a storm to come.

Will it be rain, or will it be hail
Or will it be only tornado or gale
But the storm is sure to come.

The sun is sinking far to the west
Black clouds roll to do their best
To hide the sinking sun.

The wind grows strong, the rain drops fall
Quickly they answer to natures call
As the clouds drop torrents of rain.

The storm clouds lift their angry heads
Then comes that what everyone dreads.
The hail began to fall.

Crashing and banging the thunder rolls
Lightening striking the telephone polls
As the storm plays out its rage.

Lightening shoots across the sky
lighting up both far and niegh
It's natures fireworks display.

Rain drops slow their quick decent
Storm clouds vanish out of sight.
The storm is over and gone.

The morning dawns so bright and clear
Rain drops glisten like a fallen tear,
On the fresh green trees and lawn.

Flowers bloom under fallen trees
None is arrayed like one of these
Enjoying God's bright warm sun.

Little Ostrich

Hello little Ostrich
We're happy you to see.
After over 40 days
You've of the eggshell free.

Eat little Ostrich,
Eat and drink for me.
It's very good you know,
Try it you will see.
Grow little Ostrich,
Grow and grow some more.
Very soon you'll find your head
Far above the floor.

Run little Ostrich,
Run it's good for you.
Happy healthy little birds
Will tell you it is true.

We love you little Ostrich,
We'll love and care for you.
Stick around and you will find
What I say is true.

For Danny's 8th birthday

There is a very special boy
As special as can be.
A greater boy you could not find
Just meet him you will see.

His name is Daniel Seth,
We're glad he's come to stay,
We wish him happy birthday
For he's 8 years old today.

GOD gave us this great treasure
Oh, what a wondrous gift.
We are so very thankful
In prayer our faces lift,

We love this very special boy,
And now would like to say
We love you and for you
We every day will pray.

PRAY TELL?

Have you no words? Ah think again!
Words flow space when you complain,
And fill your fellow creatures' ear
With the sad tales of all your care.

Were half the breath so vainly spent
To heaven in supplication sent,
Your cheerful song would oftener be,
"Hear what the Lord has done for me."

God Is Near!

The sun shines down on the sparking lake
Little waves play and glistens make.
Dragon flies hover in shinning blue
They're made by God, This is true.
God is near.

Flowers dance in the summer breeze
None is adorned like one of these.
Fluffy white clouds go floating by
In the bright blue summer sky.
Telling us God is near.

Below we see the song birds fly
Away down low and away up high,
Telling to all the world around,
More beautiful voice cannot be found.
That God is near.

Cheerfully the seagulls fly
Nestled in the bright blue sky,
Over the glistening azure lake
Watching for some food to take.
God is near.

Graciously the grasses bow
Beneath the farmer's favourite cow.
Little fish jump excitedly
Under the branch of a fallen tree.
Knowing God is near.

Flies and mosquitos hum contentedly
Little frog croaks, "Come play with me."
The beaver slaps his big flat tail
Under the water he then does sail.
And God is near.

Little ducks float with their heads held high
Reflected in the summer sky
Ducking their heads for a nice choice worm.
How did they know of this to learn?
Oh, God is near.

Chickens are calling , "Come gather my eggs."
Little dog barks-- it's for food he begs.
Smoke from the fire up the chimney steals
While mother is cooking the evening meal.
And God is near.

The farmer plows the grassy field
Envisioning the food that it will yield.
Tree leaves flutter in the gentle breeze
This is what the old man sees
For God is near.

The old man sits in his rocking chair
Breathing in the clear fresh air
Enjoying and counting the blessings found.
And oh the blessings did abound.
For God was near.

For the birds and the bees and the summer showers
For help that he needed in desperate hours
For strength for the path to do whats right
For the rest that he needed to have each night
Knowing that God was near.

The wind then whispered in the old mans ear
He will not cause you a needless tear
He will be with you, as He was through the years
So put away worry, Put away fears.
For God is near.

The old man smiled and he began to prayed
And this is what he had to say.
"Thank you God for all you have done
But thank you most for your beloved Son
I know – God is near.

SNOW IS COMING

Cold wind don't blow, and bring us snow
We've much to be done as I soon you will show.
The garden needs digging, carrots long to be found
The potatoes are popping right out of the ground.

The trees have all thrown their leaves on the lawn
But if north wind blows they'll soon be all gone.
The fences need fixing the wires hanging down
It won't keep the cows from wandering around.

The barn needs some fixing to keep out the snow
More lights should be added the cattle to show.
Ostrich sheds waiting for windows in walls
Siding needs finishing, door for hanging calls

When these jobs are finished
The tools hung up neatly
If come wind you must
Bringing snow and the sleet.

BLESSINGS

Our lives are full of blessings
We should be thankful for.
For daily food and ample strength
To meet our trials sore.

For clothes on our back
And shoes on our feet
And the ability to walk
Down the city street.

For eyes that can see
The grass and the trees
For the mountains and land
And the open seas.

For the computer that's stored
In the top of our head
For the safety we have
As we go to bed.

For the family and friends
And their loving careless
For all the good things
We have and can share.

And Oh for the Man
Who died on the tree
That you and I – sinners
From sin might be free.

So – don't take all this
And suffer no lack
As you journey through life
Give something back.

And Ill tell you something
Something you'll learn
When you give a smile
You'll get one in return.

Show some love and kindness
To your fellow man
This is His desire
T'is His Devine plan.

Tell others you're thankful
For the help they have been
And always remember
To Him it is seen.

While you're showing you are grateful
That you have no lack
As you journey through life
Give something back

A Tribute To My Mother

When you are gone
And basking in Heaven's glow.
Will your friends be heard to say
She was good to know?

She told me about the Saviour
And His redeeming grace
She was always there to help
With her radiant smiling face.

She was always there to offer
Encouragement every day.
And she always ready
Of the right words there to say.

When the clouds of trouble
Grew dark about her head
She always saw the lining
Of silver that they had.

She was always cheerful
Though I often wondered why
But I think it was her saviour
She had up there on high.

Oh may I with her example
A pattern for my walk
And have my feet to follow
To walk and not just talk.

PILGRIM

Oh pilgrim are you weary,
The way seem dark and long?
Life fraught with many trials
Drowning out your cheerful song?
The boisterous waves are tossing
Your ship upon the sea?
The storm clouds dark are gathering
The sun you can not see?
You feel that you are sinking
Or perhaps you've run aground
And yes you have forgotten
That you are heaven bound?
Oh call for help dear pilgrim
He wants to hear from you
He's always up there watching
And waiting for you too.
The storm clouds part so slightly
Beyond, you see the sun
And you hear that sweet soft whisper
Of the Beloved one.
"A little while, it won't be long.
'Till then keep faith
And take my hand
I'll lead you safe to
The promised land.

MAY GOD BLESS YOU

I remember the first time I saw you there
In the hospital curled up in a ball
You opened your eyes, those beautiful eyes.
It was a love affair at first sight.
I prayed that God would bless you.

I lovingly watched you as you grew
My love for you grew too.
You loved to play, to laugh and romp
But you had a serious side too.
I prayed for you as you grew.

One day you gave me a book mark you made
You drew it with such care.
I placed it in my bible, it's still there'
When I see it I am reminded to
Pray that God would bless you.

You have such a gentle caring way
So thoughtful to those around.
You loved to dream you worked so hard
At school at the farm at play
And I prayed God would bless you.

You graduated from Vermillion
Then went to Olds for collage
I realized then that there must be
A special young bride for you.
I prayed that God would bless you.

Then God sent Becca along your way
We loved her the day we met.
A helpmeet for you to walk by your side
To help in your journey through life.
I pray that God will bless you.

Make the Lord your shepherd, your guide and your
friend
In all that you do and say.
He'll guide you at work, He'll guide you at play
He'll guide you all life through.
Remember I'm praying God will bless you

50th wedding anniversary

Little did I guess
Some 50 years ago today
All the troubles we would face
Too numerous to say.
Hardships we encountered
On our journey day by day
Hardships drew us closer
To endure them come what may.
But our blessings far out numbered
The hard times we have had

Three wonderful special children
Who call us Mom and Dad.
They each in turn have chosen
A mate to love, hold dear
Then given us thirteen grandkids
Each we hold so dear.
The children we love so dearly
More dear they cannot be
We count them special blessings

And part of our family tree.
Together we have sorrowed
For loved ones gone before
Together we've lamented
Luxuries we can't afford.

Together we've rejoiced
As trials we overcame
Together we have worshipped
In Jesus Holy Name.

Together we have traveled.
Over the bumpy road of life
But never have I regretted
When I became your wife.

It's been a super journey
We've laughed and loved and cried
I count it a real blessing
To have you by my side.

WHAT A GIFT

Jesus for all mans' sins did die
His blood was shed for me
And He again went up on high
So eternal life: I'd see.

Oh Lord my heart I give to Thee
I long to look above
Thy presence Lord oh let me see
Oh, fill me with thy love.

To serve Thee with my life I fail
To live the way I should
Oh help me Lord for Thee to hale
Lord of my life I would.

Into your heart ask Him today
His blood cleanses from sin
And you will be His child always
He'll give you peace within

One day He's coming bye and bye
For all His ransomed throng
To take us with Him up on high
I pray it won't be long.

THE BOAT YARD

Fog is drifting among
The towering masts
Dew is dripping
From the rails so fast.

The Mourning dove coos
Her wake up call
She seems to be saying
Come get up all.

People who are walking
To their morning shower
Quietly call greetings
At this early hour.

The aroma of coffee
Is in the air
Folks quietly visiting
Here and there.

The sun will be coming
Out in plain view
Chasing the fog
As the day starts anew.

The air will be filled
With noises it seems
Every one is chasing
Their personal dreams.

Sanding a bottom
Fixing a prop
Polishing their boats
From bottom to top.

Fixing a mast
That came off in the storm
Sanding it, painting it
'Til it's in great form

Motors that are broken
Are being repaired
Dreams for the future
Are being shared.

Life in the yard
Has been such fun
But now it is time
To sit in the sun!

I feel like Noah
Out here in the yard
It's starting to rain
And my boat's on the hard.

THERE WAS A WEDDING

It was commonly reported
There was a wedding here today.
What? Right here in the boat yard?
Some would even dare to say.

Yes right here in the boat yard
All with friends that they have met!
We were all happy to be here
How lucky can you get?

The bride, she was so pretty
Her little dress was white.
Becca made her blue bouquet.
She fashioned it just right.

Baby's breath adorned her hair
Was placed upon her head.
Mikey walked her down the isle.
"You're special Mom, he said.

Oh she looked so pretty
Walking down the isle.
We were so happy to be here.
We couldn't help but smile.

Nathalie and Lenard led the way
As he walked her down the isle
To stand beneath the boat lift
Proctor placed there for a while.

Kim had made it fancy
With ribbons and balloons.
It was so big and lofty
It would have filled a room.

Don took her gently by the arm
And stood there by her side
Our lives will be together now
Hang on for a great ride.

They pledged to love each other
And even shed a tear.
And hoped to be together
For many a happy year.

The preacher said he joined them
He joined them now for life.
He said a few more things, then
He called them man and wife.

Yes there was a wedding here today
A wedding in the yard.
The yard where all the boats have come
To put upon the hard.

Ever will I be thankful we
Were there to share the day
And a little of the joy they shared
On this their wedding day!

Jim and Dora McPeek
My Parents
(written for the Schobert history book by Dora)

We were married November 5, 1925 at five o'clock, a very cold and damp day, at my parents' home. The Schoberts had finished harvest but the McPeeks had not. Not much pomp, very plain. I bought a silky sand coloured dress. The dress had a small collar and was long sleeved, mid-calf length and straight. My bouquet was pink and white carnations. I wore a string of pearls and black suede shoes. Jim wore a dark suit. My brother Pete and sister Margaret were our attendants. The minister was from Congress. It was a very brief Ceremony, just the vows. We stood with our back to the family and my mother sang a solo in German while we signed the register. Jim's brother Ben accompanied my mother with difficulty as he had never seen or practiced the song beforehand. After signing the register, the minister introduced us as Mr. and Mrs. James McPeek and everyone lined up to congratulate us and shake hands. At six o'clock we had a big meal of roast chicken and turkey. Two tables were pushed together and covered with a tablecloth. The guests were: Jim's family, except Dewey; my family except Mick and Buck; the minister and his wife; my friends and schoolmates Grace, Lillian and Mildred Johnson; and three of Jim's friends. It was a very crowded house that day. Eric or Walter gave Dad a drink before the wedding. Dad was very talkative and wanted to argue about Biblical points. Normally he was very quiet. About nine o'clock Jim and I left by the McPeek Model T truck with the whole McPeek clan. The next morning Jim went back to work in the harvest.

We lived on the James Alvin McPeek farm, (north of Melaval about six miles), until 1927. Then we bought a farm near Mazenod, right near Palmer and we lived there two years.

They had 9 children:
1) **Grace Evelyn McPeek** - B: August 1, 1926 in Melaval, Sask.

2) **Ruth Magdalene McPeek** - B: January 2, 1928 in Melaval, Sask.

3) **William Bud McPeek** - B:April 15, 1929 in Melaval, Sask.

4) **Irene Udora McPeek** - B: March 4, 1931 in Wood Mountain, Sask.

5) **Hazel Audrey McPeek** - B: January 26, 1933 in Wood Mountain, Sask.

6) **Shirley Mae McPeek** - B: August 8, 1935 in Lanigan, Sask.

7) **Earl Ralph McPeek** - B: January 31, 1938 in Mazenod, Sask.

8) **George Herbert McPeek** - B: May 19, 1941 in Coronach, Sask.

9) **Linda Faye McPeek** - B: December 31, 1944 in Coronach, Sask.

They also lived at Mazenod, Sk, Wood Mountain, Sk, Lanigan, Sk, Mazenod, Sk, Coronach, Sk (farm), Coronach, Sk (house across from the school), Coronach Senior Home.

ABOUT THE AUTHOR

Shirley Mae (McPeek) Heslop was born in 1935 in southern Saskatchewan to a poor farming family. She was 6th of 9 children. Shirley wishes that she had gotten to know more about her mother and father's history before they passed away. Because of this she decided to write down some of her childhood memories for her children and grandchildren.

This book had its beginnings while she was sitting in her hospital bed following a stroke. Unable to speak or even read, she wrote in a notebook and had her husband read what she had written, to make sure that it was making sense. Eventually she fought her way back to health. Shirley currently lives in Airdrie, Alberta with her husband of 63 years, Alan.

68384084R00128

Made in the USA
Middletown, DE
16 September 2019